AMERICAN
WAR LIBRARY

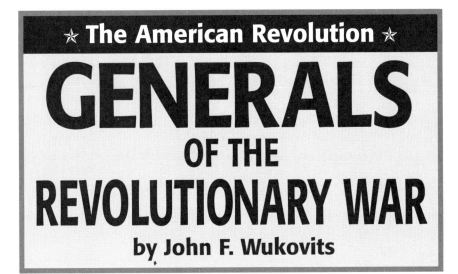

★ The American Revolution ★

GENERALS
OF THE
REVOLUTIONARY WAR

by John F. Wukovits

Titles in the American War Library series include:

The American Revolution
Generals of the Revolutionary War
Life of a Soldier in
  Washington's Army
Patriots of the Revolutionary War
Primary Sources
Strategic Battles
Weapons of War

The Civil War
Leaders of the North and South
Life Among the Soldiers and
  Cavalry
Lincoln and the Abolition of
  Slavery
Primary Sources
Strategic Battles
Weapons of War

World War I
Flying Aces
Leaders and Generals
Life in the Trenches
Primary Sources
Strategic Battles
Weapons of War

World War II
Hitler and the Nazis
Kamikazes
Leaders and Generals
Life as a POW
Life of an American Soldier in
  Europe

Primary Sources
Strategic Battles in Europe
Strategic Battles in the Pacific
The War at Home
Weapons of War

The Cold War
The Battlefront: Other Nations
Containing the Communists:
  America's Foreign Entanglements
The Cold War Ends: 1980 to the
  Present
Espionage
The Homefront
Political Leaders
Primary Sources
An Uneasy Peace: 1945–1980
Weapons of Peace: The Nuclear
  Arms Race

The Vietnam War
History of U.S. Involvement
The Home Front: Americans
  Protest the War
Leaders and Generals
Life as a POW
Life of an American Soldier
Primary Sources
Weapons of War

The Persian Gulf War
Leaders and Generals
Life of an American Soldier
The War Against Iraq
Weapons of War

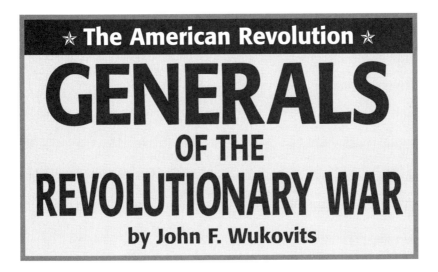

☆ The American Revolution ☆

GENERALS
OF THE
REVOLUTIONARY WAR

by John F. Wukovits

LUCENT
BOOKS ®

THOMSON
™

San Diego • Detroit • New York • San Fr⋯   ⋯rville, Maine • London • Munich

© 2003 by Lucent Books. Lucent Books is an imprint of The Gale Group, Inc., a division of Thomson Learning, Inc.

Lucent Books® and Thomson Learning™ are trademarks used herein under license.

For more information, contact
Lucent Books
27500 Drake Rd.
Farmington Hills, MI 48331-3535
Or you can visit our Internet site at http://www.gale.com

LIBRARY OF CONGRESS CATALOGING-IN-PUBLICATION DATA

Wukovits, John F., 1944–
    Generals of the Revolutionary War / by John F. Wukovits.
        p. cm. — (American war library. American Revolution series)
Summary: Profiles seven heroes of the American Revolution, looking especially at the leadership qualities that led to their military successes.
Includes bibliographical references and index.
        ISBN 1-59018-219-7 (hardback : alk. paper)
    1. United States—History—Revolution, 1775–1783—Biography—Juvenile literature.
2. Generals—United States—Biography—Juvenile literature. 3. Generals—Great Britain—Biography—Juvenile literature. [1. United States—History—Revolution, 1775–1783—Biography. 2. Generals.] I. Title. II. Series.
    E206 .W85 2003
    973.3'092'2—dc21
                                                                                        2002010426

Printed in the United States of America

★ Contents ★

A Nation Forged by War

The United States, like many nations, was forged and defined by war. Despite Benjamin Franklin's opinion that "There never was a good war or a bad peace," the United States owes its very existence to the War of Independence, one to which Franklin wholeheartedly subscribed. The country forged by war in 1776 was tempered and made stronger by the Civil War in the 1860s.

The Texas Revolution, the Mexican-American War, and the Spanish-American War expanded the country's borders and gave it overseas possessions. These wars made the United States a world power, but this status came with a price, as the nation became a key but reluctant player in both World War I and World War II.

Each successive war further defined the country's role on the world stage. Following World War II, U.S. foreign policy redefined itself to focus on the role of defender, not only of the freedom of its own citizens but also of the freedom of people everywhere. During the cold war that followed World War II until the collapse of the Soviet Union, defending the world meant fighting communism. This goal, manifested in the Korean and Vietnam conflicts, proved elusive, and soured the American public on its achievability. As the United States emerged as the world's sole superpower, American foreign policy has been guided less by national interest and more on protecting international human rights. But as involvement in Somalia and Kosovo proves, this goal has been equally elusive.

As a result, the country's view of itself changed. Bolstered by victories in World Wars I and II, Americans first relished the role of protector. But, as war followed war in a seemingly endless procession, Americans began to doubt their leaders, their motives, and themselves. The Vietnam War especially caused people to question the validity of sending its young people to die in places where they were not particularly wanted and for people who did not seem especially grateful.

While the most obvious changes brought about by America's wars have been geopolitical in nature, many other aspects of society have been touched. War often does not bring about change directly, but acts instead like the catalyst in a chemical reaction, accelerating changes already in progress.

Some of these changes have been societal. The role of women in the United States had been slowly changing, but World War II put thousands into the workforce and into uniform. They might have gone back to being housewives after the war, but equality, once experienced, would not be forgotten.

Likewise, wars have accelerated technological change. The necessity for faster airplanes and a more destructive bomb led to the development of jet planes and nuclear energy. Artificial fibers developed for parachutes in the 1940s were used in the clothing of the 1950s.

Lucent Books' American War Library covers key wars in the development of the nation. Each war is covered in several volumes, to allow for more detail, context, and to provide volumes on often neglected subjects, such as the kamikazes of World War II, or weapons used in the Civil War. As with all Lucent Books, notes, annotated bibliographies, and appendixes such as glossaries give students a launching point for further research. In addition, sidebars and archival photographs enhance the text. Together, each volume in the American War Library will aid students in understanding how America's wars have shaped and changed its politics, economics, and society.

The Qualities of Leadership

Each man selected for this book enjoyed success to some degree, else they would not be remembered more than two hundred years after they lived. They did not achieve it in equal measure. In fact, only one man profiled—George Washington—can be said to have attained unparalleled triumph, and even he experienced early failures and periods of near desperation. John Paul Jones enjoyed considerable success at sea, yet he lacked a stable home. The other five experienced tumultuous mixtures of defeat and victory, glory and ignominy, fame and notoriety.

What made them succeed or fail? Within the careers of these seven individuals, certain patterns appear that help answer the question of what makes a man a talented military leader.

Indecision Versus Determination

Two factors that affect a battle's outcome are the opposite qualities of indecision and determination. So often in the American Revolution a commander's indecision—his inability to make a choice and to stick with it—determined the course of battle. As commander in chief of all British forces in North America, British general William Howe, an able officer when in charge of smaller units, repeatedly shrank from ordering his men forward when one more push might have wiped out George Washington's army. After pushing Washington out of Long Island and after victories at Brandywine and Germantown, instead of pursuing the fleeing revolutionary forces, Howe halted his men and settled into winter quarters, each time handing Washington a new chance to reorganize and continue the fight. On the American side, General Horatio Gates's hesitant performance at Camden led to one of the worst defeats in the Revolution.

While indecision produces little of value, determination can frequently decide the battle's outcome. Even those commanders profiled in this book whose careers might be said to be failures are remembered for moments of greatness on the battlefield, usually because they conveyed the attitude to their troops that nothing was going to stop them, that they would triumph no matter what obstacle lay in their path. From the very beginning, John Paul Jones let his men know that he would place his ship in the heat of

Revolutionary War musicians proudly play in A.M. Willard's rendition, *Yankee Doodle 1776.*

the action and fight until their opponent had surrendered. Even though the task appeared impossible, William Howe led a small force up the heights in front of Quebec, surprised the French, and helped gain a crucial victory for the British during the French and Indian War. Though he faced many low points throughout the Revolution, George Washington's determination was the glue that held the Continental army together until aid from France helped secure a triumph.

Reputation Versus Reality

Two other factors that go hand in hand are the concern that some commanders had for their own reputations and the willingness of others to forsake glory for the good of their men. British generals Charles Cornwallis and John Burgoyne frequently measured an operation's value according to what it might do for them with their superiors in London. When critics pointed out their shortcomings, both either asked for official inquiries to clear their names or engaged in heated arguments over the placement of credit for victory or blame for defeat. Benedict Arnold was so concerned over his reputation and glory, which he believed had suffered at the hands of jealous American officers, that

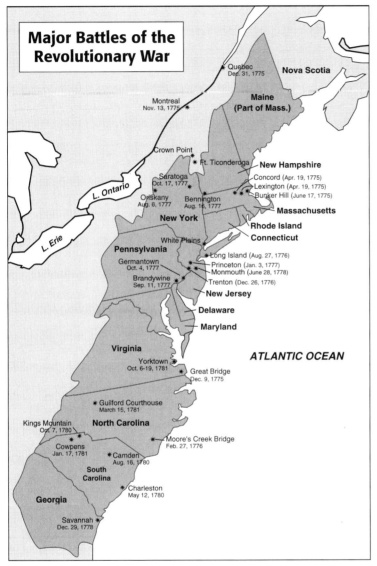

Major Battles of the Revolutionary War

Jones, not surprisingly the two who most achieved success in the Revolution.

Instead of concentrating on their careers and fame, the most talented commanders were often those who thought first of their men. Washington endured the hardships of Valley Forge with his men, and he sent a continuous stream of letters to the Continental Congress begging for more supplies and uniforms. John Paul Jones, who could be a harsh commander, fought shoulder to shoulder with his sailors. This willingness to share in the war's miseries created a sense of unity among the officers and men that helped achieve success. Soldiers and sailors will fight harder for an officer who willingly places his life on the line for their sake.

Overconfidence Versus Desperation

The final pairing of values most emphasizes why Britain lost the American Revolution. Almost every major British officer assumed their nation's army, ranked among the most powerful military machines formed in European history, would easily defeat Washington

he switched sides in the middle of the war. Formerly a brilliant leader, Arnold receded to the background once he allowed ambition and fame to dominate his thoughts. The only two who disdained glory and honors were Washington and

and the Americans. This overconfidence produced an arrogance that led the British to conclude the Americans, while gallant fighters in the frontier, could pose no threat to the disciplined ranks that England would throw at them. British officers repeatedly went into battle as if they had already won. This mental outlook contributed to England's fall as much as any cannonball or battle, for it led to mistakes in planning campaigns and in orchestrating them once the conflict started.

The Americans, on the other hand, possessed no overwhelming advantage, and in no small measure this helped them attain victory. When an officer and an army fight out of desperation, when there is nothing to lose, the outcome can often be favorable. The commander accepts risks that he might normally avoid; he considers strategy that he otherwise might dismiss. Most important, he adopts unconventional measures that catch the enemy by surprise. Desperation, when harnessed wisely, can be a powerful element in success, as was shown by Washington at Trenton, by Benedict Arnold at Valcour Island, and by Jones in his duel with the *Serapis*.

The seven profiles in this collection show that, in wartime, the side that wins may not be the more powerful or the better equipped. It simply needs the better leaders and the more powerful motivation.

Chapter 1

George Washington: Man for All the People

Every military leader profiled in this book contributed in one way or another to the Revolutionary War's outcome. Most performed their duties leading men on the battlefield, but one—George Washington—had an impact far beyond the boundaries of war. His actions affected not only the soldiers he commanded and the officers with whom he worked but also civilians in every state.

A Comfortable Life

Born February 22, 1732, in eastern Virginia, George Washington knew little hardship as a youth. While his family could never lay claim to being the wealthiest in the region, they certainly enjoyed a pleasant lifestyle. His father, Augustine, owned ten thousand acres of choice farmland and fifty slaves. After a first marriage, which produced two sons and a daughter, ended with his wife's death, Augustine remarried to Mary Ball.

Their son, George, loved riding horses and shooting rifles. Impressive looking because of his calm demeanor and his above-average height, Washington intended to do well in whatever he selected as a profession. In his teenage years he carefully penned a set of rules into a notebook, reminding him how he should behave. Since Washington believed in the importance of treating people with respect and in behaving properly, this list became something of a model for him to follow. Among the admonitions was a reminder to never clean his teeth when at the dinner table, to pay attention when another person speaks, to rise when others enter the room, and to avoid drumming his fingers on the table.

He at first expected to follow his two half brothers to England, where they were enrolled in some of the finest schools, but his father's death when George was eleven years old ended that hope. His father's will provided for an

In this painting, young George Washington displays his honesty and admits fault for cutting down a cherry tree.

eventual bounty, however, by setting aside twenty-five hundred acres of land, a family house, and ten slaves to be delivered to Washington on his twenty-first birthday.

Washington intended to be an officer in the British navy, but his mother wanted him closer to home and forbade it. He studied reading, writing, and mathematics, then entered the promising field of surveying the western frontier lands. In 1749 he became the official surveyor of Culpepper County, Virginia, and headed out to designate the boundary lines of the region. An unforeseen benefit of this work was that Washington gained valuable knowledge of the wilderness that he would later use in military campaigns. Washington also earned enough money

with his surveying work to purchase 453 acres of land.

When not roaming about in the frontier, Washington spent a great amount of time at Mount Vernon, the estate of his half brother Lawrence. When Lawrence died of a disease in 1752, Washington inherited not only Mount Vernon, but also his brother's post as an officer in the county militia.

Action Against the French

It did not take Washington long to use his newly found position as military officer.

When France started to build forts in the Ohio Valley—land claimed by the British—Virginia governor Robert Dinwiddie formed an expedition to deliver a message demanding that the French leave the valley. In 1753 Washington volunteered to lead the soldiers through the wilderness to hand over the ultimatum, which he did after a strenuous fifty-two-day trek across five hundred miles of forests, rivers, and swamps. He received little in return for his effort except French derision. When Washington handed Dinwiddie's message to the French commander, the officer said, "As to the summons you send me to retire, I do not think myself obliged to obey it."[1]

Faced by a numerically superior unit of French soldiers, Washington had no choice but to make the long voyage back to Virginia and report to Dinwiddie. The Virginia executive promptly raised a stronger expedition, with Washington as second in command, and gave orders to force out the French.

After another arduous march, Washington led an attack on a small French

As a newly appointed officer, George Washington (right) sets out to warn the French of the Britons' distaste for their Ohio Valley occupation.

post near modern-day Pittsburgh. The brief skirmish, in which Washington's men killed ten French soldiers and captured the rest, formed the opening battle of the French and Indian War, referred to by the British as the Seven Years' War. To shield his men against the inevitable French counterattack, Washington hurried to construct a rude fort. Fort Necessity offered shelter, but rainwater flooded the inexperienced commander's trenches. In addition, since Washington had failed to clear the area around the fort sufficiently, the French were able to hide among the trees and fire from close range.

The battle opened on July 3, 1754. Within one hour the French had overrun the fort and killed thirty of Washington's men. The next day, despite putting up a valiant struggle against superior odds, Washington surrendered the remaining garrison. He was permitted to lead his men out of the fort and return to Virginia.

So far, Washington's military career consisted of delivering an ultimatum that had been ignored and a defeat, but the determined young officer returned for more in 1755.

He volunteered to join an expedition of two thousand men led by British general Edward Braddock against French-held Fort Duquesne, now Pittsburgh. Before the men reached their destination, the French stunned them with a surprise attack. Again, Washington fought bravely, even though two horses were shot

out from underneath him and bullets tore his coat. His courage could not alter the outcome, however, as the outnumbered British fell in scores. By the end of the battle, almost one thousand British lay dead or wounded, including the mortally injured Braddock. Washington helped lead the remnants back to safety in Virginia.

The first phase of Washington's military career ended in 1759 when he resigned from the military and married the widowed Martha Custis. Content to be away from the fighting after his skirmishes against the French, Washington tended to Mount Vernon and served for fifteen years as a member of the Virginia House of Burgesses. Soon, however, the summons of military duty beckoned him back into uniform.

"Avoid a General Action"

Soon after the battles at Lexington and Concord that launched the American Revolution, the Continental Congress searched for a man to organize, train, and lead the army that would oppose the British. Most politicians had Washington's name at the top of their lists. The tall, handsome, regal Virginian not only fit the image of a successful military leader, but his years in military service had made him one of the most experienced commanders in the colonies.

Thus Washington faced a monumental task when he arrived in Boston and took command of the Continental Army

on July 3, 1775, only two weeks after Bunker Hill. The army lacked supplies in all areas, especially wagons, gunpowder, and ammunition. Pay was low and food was bad.

Unless he recruited more soldiers or persuaded the original two thousand men who had signed on to extend their terms of service, within a short time Washington would be a leader without an army, for the men had agreed to fight for only a few months. In any event, the colonial soldiers were inexperienced, ill-trained, and hardly prepared for battle against the finest European army.

Washington's primary task in the war's early period was thus not to endanger his forces until they had enough man-

Washington takes command of the Continental Army.

power and training to meet the British. He had first to create an army, complete with experienced officers and supplies, and then to keep it intact until it found its bearings. He wrote to the president of the Continental Congress, "We should on all occasions avoid a general action, or put anything to the risque, unless compelled by a necessity, into which we ought never to be drawn."[2]

As a result, Washington decided he would not permit the British to lure him into an open fight in which the superior British training might dominate. He would, instead, roam about the countryside where he would avoid any British force sent to locate him, striking only if a favorable opportunity presented itself. Thus he was willing, though not happy, to yield New York and Pennsylvania to the British so he could maintain his army in the field.

Washington knew other factors stood on his side, however. The men might be ill-trained frontiersmen, but they fought for their own homes and soil, an advantage the professional British army could not claim. Washington would be moving about familiar lands, while the British had to coordinate campaigns with superiors three thousand miles across the Atlantic Ocean. Thus while still in Boston he was able to score an impressive success by moving a group of captured cannon to nearby heights overlooking the city. This unexpected action stunned the British, who now had to make a hasty retreat from the city to avoid being subject to murderous barrages.

Fighting on Eastern Long Island

The scene of fighting switched to New York, where General William Howe landed a large force of soldiers intent on controlling the important region. Washington hastened to Long Island with twenty-eight thousand men to block the advance. Yet, initially, the British commander outwitted the American, sending a part of his force to outflank Washington's Long Island encampment. The move forced Washington to order his men

to fall back to fortifications near Brooklyn, along the East River, where the colonists faced a complete defeat should the British press their attack.

Washington attempted to rally his men by telling them, "I will not ask any man to go further than I do. I will fight as long as I have a leg or an arm."[3] In case those stirring words failed to work, Washington confided to two colonels that he carried two loaded pistols and would not hesitate to shoot the first men who tried to retreat.

Thinking that Washington would willingly surrender rather than face disaster, however, Howe halted his advance. The delay handed the American commander an opportunity to extricate his army from the trap. That night, while Howe and the British relaxed in their tents, Washington collected every available boat and, masked by an opportune fog, moved his ninety-five hundred men to the Manhattan side of the mile-wide East River. Washington waited until every soldier was safely aboard a boat before stepping into one himself.

On September 15, 1776, the British struck across the river and began chasing Washington, who ordered one brief attack on September 16 in hopes of delaying his pursuers. Then, moving northwest, the Americans crossed the Hudson River and swerved down into New Jersey. On December 7, Washington led his weary army across the Delaware River into Pennsylvania. Howe, again overcautiously

General Washington leads his army's retreat to East River fortifications after being outwitted by British general William Howe.

assuming Washington had finished his fighting for the winter, left a small garrison at Trenton, New Jersey, to keep an eye on the Americans while he led the rest of his men into comfortable winter quarters.

Washington had erred in this early campaign. Had he sent out adequate reconnaissance troops, he may have discovered the British flanking maneuver in time to halt it. Like most everyone else on the American side, though, Washington was learning while on the job and while facing the most professional army from Europe. Mistakes were bound to happen, but Washington was determined not to repeat them.

A Christmas Gift in Trenton

One thing he dearly needed was a reason for his soldiers to remain. Many—cold, weary, poorly paid—had openly talked about leaving once their terms of service expired.

Already, Washington's numbers had shrunk to only three thousand men. The commander needed a reason for these men to remain and for others to enlist and increase the ranks. He confided to his assistant, Joseph Reed, that his numbers stood so low he had to take a daring chance, if one should come along.

He found it at Trenton, New Jersey, where fifteen hundred Hessians—soldiers from Germany hired by England to fight in America—were quartered. A spy informed Washington that the Hessians planned to celebrate Christmas with copious amounts of rum and that they would be in no condition to fight the next day. Washington saw an opportunity to make a quick strike and record a much-needed victory for the American cause.

Before he led his men across the Delaware River, Washington ordered that the famous words of Thomas Paine, recorded in his pamphlet, *American Crisis,* be read to every unit. The stirring words reminded everyone of the task before them. "These are the times that try men's souls," wrote Paine. "The summer soldier and the sunshine patriot will shrink from the service of their country. But he who stands it now deserves the love and thanks of man and woman."[4]

Washington's three thousand men, looking more like a ragged army of hoodlums in their tattered clothes and shoeless feet wrapped in cloth, crossed the river in boats, then split into two columns for the nine-mile march to Trenton. Frigid temperatures, snow, and sleet bombarded the men along the route and made footing treacherous, but by the early morning hours of December 26, they stood ready to attack. The Hessians, sleeping off their revelry, had no idea

an enemy force had moved within striking distance.

This and overconfidence sealed their doom. When a soldier earlier remarked to the Hessian commanding officer, Colonel Johann Gottlieb Rall, the possibility that the Americans could attack, he replied scornfully, "Fiddlesticks! Those clodhoppers will not attack us! And should they do so, we will simply fall on them and rout them."[5]

When Washington's two columns attacked, many Hessians, still feeling the effects of their Christmas festivities, had trouble defending themselves. Rall stumbled out of his quarters and shouted to his sleeping men, but few answered the order. In less than one hour the Americans killed or wounded one hundred Hessians, including a mortally stricken Rall, while taking nine hundred prisoner. There were five American casualties: two dead and three wounded.

Washington followed this brilliant assault with a smaller one a few days later when he defeated another British force, this time at nearby Princeton. With two victories, Washington turned his men around and headed for northern New Jersey, where they went into winter quarters.

The double triumphs at Trenton and Princeton had the effect Washington desired. Soldiers lined up to reenlist for another tour, while more joined from the civilian ranks. Citizens in New York, Pennsylvania, and New England celebrated, church bells rang out the news,

Washington guides his men across the Delaware River on December 26, 1777, to attack unsuspecting Hessian mercenaries hired by the British.

and American resolve soared. Washington's ragtag army had inflicted stinging losses on the best Europe had to offer. One British observer gloomily stated that the Americans were "all liberty mad again."[6]

Washington had once again proven his worth as a commander. In the war's opening phases, he kept the American army intact by refusing to allow the British an opportunity to destroy it in battle. Then, when morale most needed a lift, he provided it with his daring plans against Trenton and Princeton. What made Washington so valuable was that he excelled as strategist and leader even when all about him appeared lost.

A Period of Discontent

These attributes would come more into play over the next few years, as Washington faced disaster and disappointment in a variety of ways. After moving into winter quarters, in 1777, Washington attempted to prevent Howe from seizing Philadelphia, the American seat of government. Two setbacks in the fall of 1777, in Pennsylvania and at Brandywine and Germantown, opened the road to Philadelphia, which Howe entered on September 26.

At the same time, Washington marched his men into winter quarters at a nearby location—Valley Forge.

The worst winter of the Revolution unfolded in the dismal valley. Men huddled close to one another for warmth against the numbing cold and scoured the land for anything to eat. Two thousand men died and another two thousand deserted during this winter, leaving Washington almost in despair.

A bright spot came from Baron von Steuben, a German officer who had traveled to America to help in the fight for freedom. An expert military instructor, Steuben continually drilled the men in battlefield movements and strategy. By the time spring arrived, the remaining troops had been molded into a well-disciplined unit.

Shortly after leaving Valley Forge in the spring of 1778, Washington faced the British at the Battle of Monmouth Court House, New Jersey. Washington handed control of the battle to a subordinate, Charles Lee, but the hesitant general mismanaged the affair. When Washington learned that some of the soldiers were retreating, he rode up to Lee, angrily asked what was happening, then took over command of the battle. Washington halted the retreat, but night ended the affair as a draw.

For the next two years most of the action shifted to the southern states, where the British hoped to eliminate American opposition before diverting their attention once more toward Washington.

The End at Yorktown

As the British and American armies maneuvered about the southern countryside, Washington received an opportunity to trap a large force. The British decided

German military officer Baron von Steuben was known for drilling Washington's army in battlefield strategy.

to move out of the Carolinas and advance into Virginia, and sent more than seven thousand men under Charles Cornwallis to Yorktown, a city along the coastline. Washington dispatched one army of twelve hundred men to engage Cornwallis, under the Marquis de Lafayette, a French aristocrat who had volunteered his service in the cause of American liberty.

Washington then attempted to arrange a rendezvous with the French navy. If the French could blockade Cornwallis's route at sea, Washington would move south to join Lafayette and bottle up the British on land. When the French commander agreed, Washington marched into Virginia, entrenched before Yorktown, and began a huge bombardment of British lines.

By September 1781, fifteen thousand American and French soldiers pinned Cornwallis's army along the York River at Yorktown. A monthlong barrage so reduced the British defenses that, on October 17, Cornwallis asked for a truce. With this surrender, the British army in North America had been defeated, even though the treaty formalizing the outcome would not be signed until September 1783.

A tired Washington, eager to return to his beloved Mount Vernon, said farewell to his officers on December 4, 1783, at a dinner in New York. As he slowly traveled home, in nearly every city through which he passed, people turned out to welcome the commander. Though he appreciated his countrymen's affection, Washington yearned to be once more in the safe confines of home.

Leader of the Nation

Rare among leaders at the top level, Washington reveled in the quiet life of a farmer. When King George III of England heard that Washington, his opponent in the recent war, planned to retire to his farm, the king labeled him the greatest man in the world. Washington built his farm holdings until he owned six different farms with more than two hundred slaves.

He also loved reading, reflecting on life, and welcoming visitors, although the latter occupation could, at times, weary him. Anyone who traveled near Mount Vernon seemed compelled to stop by, and the courteous Washington could never bring himself to send them away. He wrote in his diary in June 1785, eighteen months after he arrived home, "Dined with only Mrs. Washington, which I believe is the first instance of it since my retirement from public life."[7]

A normal existence was not to be his, however. Since the end of the Revolution in 1783, the nation had struggled under a dismal political arrangement called the Articles of Confederation, in which individual states, instead of the federal government, held most of the power. Without authority to tax its citizens, the government could not maintain a military or organize departments to run the nation efficiently. Within months, most of the

With help from the French, Washington (center, right) plans a major assault on the British at Yorktown.

nation's influential politicians, such as Benjamin Franklin and James Madison, saw the need to reform the articles.

In 1787 a Constitutional Convention was called to create an improved central government. Virginia selected Washington as its delegate, and even though the general would have preferred to remain at Mount Vernon, he accepted the responsibility to help serve the nation.

The convention convened in Philadelphia in May 1787. For four months, some of the most noted thinkers in North America debated the type of government needed. The document devised by the convention, what is now the Constitution of the United States, did not please everyone, but Washington approved. He believed that the men had fashioned the wisest instrument of government upon which they could agree and believed the alternative was the breakup of the nation.

The approval of nine of the thirteen former colonies was needed for the Constitution to take effect. This laborious procedure occupied another year or more.

When the Constitution was ratified, Washington learned that he had been unanimously selected to serve as the nation's first president. On April 30, 1789, he took the oath of office as president, with John Adams serving as his vice president.

Washington realized the vast importance of his conduct in this office, for which no precedents had been established. The steps Washington took, the rules he enforced, the men he included in government would establish a pattern that his successors might feel bound to follow. The Constitution gave him great room to make decisions, such as how to form a group of advisers, so he took this task seriously. As his friend and fellow politician James Madison wrote, "We are in a wilderness without a single footstep to guide us."[8]

Washington's initial moves proved sound. As his top advisers he gathered the brightest men in the land, such as Thomas Jefferson and Alexander Hamilton, without regard for whether he agreed with all their political beliefs. He then spent most of his first four years overseeing the setting up of the different departments of government and the court system and asking Congress to pass tax laws to finance the government.

Washington directs a ratification session of the 1787 Constitutional Convention.

A Second Term

After a four-year term, Washington preferred to retire once again, but advisers talked him out of it. Jefferson pointed out that Washington, still beloved for his work in the Revolution and unstained by political battles, was the one man in the nation that both the North and South would accept as leader. He reluctantly put his dreams of retirement to Mount Vernon on hold for another term, and on March 4, 1793, he and John Adams were again sworn into office.

Washington faced a severe crisis in his second term when farmers in Pennsylvania refused to pay a new national tax on whiskey. They tarred and feathered local tax collectors and threatened force, should anyone attempt to implement the law.

Washington correctly saw this as a grave challenge to the power of the federal government, so he personally led fifteen thousand soldiers to the region. The sight of the war hero, again resplendent in military uniform, reawakened feelings of patriotism in the farmers, who yielded without a fight. By suppressing this so-called Whiskey Rebellion, Washington had emphasized to his own nation and to a watching world that the federal government would enforce the laws enacted by the people's elected representatives. As

he wrote to a friend, the affair proved that "under no form of government will the laws be better supported, liberty and property better secured, or happiness more effectually dispensed to mankind"[9] than under the present system of government.

Last Years of a Hero

Finally, as his eight years as president neared an end, Washington looked to a more placid lifestyle. Weary of the political battles between Hamilton and Jefferson, Washington announced that he would not seek a third term. The exhausted warrior stepped away from his final battlefield and headed to Mount Vernon.

In July 1799 Washington made out his will, including one clause stipulating that upon his death, his slaves were to be given their freedom. On December 12, 1799, he rode about his plantation during a snowstorm. Afterward, instead of changing into a fresh suit of clothes for dinner, Washington ate while still dressed in his wet clothes. When he developed a sore throat the next day, physicians were called in for treatment, but nothing they did could help the dying statesman. After giving final instructions about the disposal of his properties, Washington died on December 14, 1799.

Chapter 2

William Howe: Hesitant Leader

The career of Sir William Howe, Britain's commander in chief in North America for three of the war's most crucial years, contains bravery and stoutheartedness in early operations, but reflects hesitation and doubt in later maneuvers. He stared at repeated opportunities to squash Washington's poorly trained forces, but each time allowed them to slip away and live to fight again. When he returned to England in 1778, instead of reporting to the king's ministers that he had suppressed dissident action in North America, he had to explain that the rebellious troops led by Washington not only remained intact, but with further training posed an even more serious threat to the British army.

A Career in the Military

William Howe was born on August 10, 1729, to the viscount Howe and his wife, Mary Sophia. Howe's aristocratic background contained influential connec-

tions, for his grandmother had been a mistress of King George I. These ties to the royal family helped Howe fashion a successful military career.

After attending Eton College, an elite preparatory school even then, Howe entered the military on September 18, 1746, as an officer in the Duke of Cumberland's Light Dragoons, a unit of cavalry. The next year he was promoted to lieutenant and sent to the continent to fight against France in the War of the Austrian Succession. Through distinguished service, by 1750 Howe gained promotion to captain and forged a close friendship with a man who would become one of England's most renowned military leaders, Major James Wolfe.

In 1758, two years after being made a major, Howe sailed to North America for his country's war with the French and their Native American allies. He quickly gained distinction with his talent for thoroughly training his men and for bold

British commander in chief William Howe sits astride his steed.

that brought him acclaim through much of England. Pitted in the French and Indian War's most crucial contest, the fighting in front of Quebec, Howe boldly led an advance party of twenty-four soldiers up the steep Heights of Abraham, surprised the French guards detailed to prevent a British force from approaching from that avenue, then held the position against numerous French assaults until General Wolfe's main army could scale the heights and assemble for battle. After Wolfe attacked, Howe took charge of four hundred men and blocked the route of two thousand French troops attempting to join the fray. Another officer wrote to a government official that Howe was "unsurpassed in activity, bravery, and experience, and beloved by his troops."[10]

In part due to Howe's stellar leadership, the British victory at Quebec helped cement that nation's hold on North America. At the same time France, which once commanded an enormous frontier empire in the region, was nudged closer to a complete withdrawal.

Howe added to his luster by participating in other victories in 1760 and in

leadership, proving his willingness to risk the same dangers faced by his men. His friend Wolfe, now a general, stated that Howe's Fifty-eighth Foot Regiment was the best-trained and most efficiently led unit in North America.

The next year Howe, now a lieutenant colonel, participated in the action

1762, and by proving the effectiveness of light infantry, units of soldiers carrying little equipment that moved with lightning speed. By the war's end the following year, Howe stood out as a leading contender for high command in the British army.

Before the Revolution

Howe fulfilled that promise by becoming, in rapid order, the commander of the Forty-sixth Foot in Ireland, the lieutenant governor of the Isle of Wight, and major general in 1772. His future seemed assured.

At the same time his military career blossomed, Howe held a political office. Following his brother George's 1758 death in combat in Massachusetts, Howe inherited his place as a member of Parliament representing the citizens of Nottingham, a post he held until 1780. Though not an active politician—in those days, officers often used service in Parliament as a means of promoting a military career—Howe opposed harsh measures against the colonies. He believed the Americans were his brethren, hence Englishmen, and that every Englishman had an unbreakable bond under the king. In addition, Howe developed ties with North America from his service against the French. He loved the land and the people, a feeling that was further solidified when the Massachusetts Assembly erected a monument to honor his fallen brother, George.

When serving in combat or training his troops, Howe followed a rigid system of command. He asked the best of his troops and promised the same effort in return. However, when in London for his Parliamentary duties, a more relaxed Howe preferred to gamble, drink, and accompany beautiful women to parties.

His London service ended on February 21, 1775, when Howe received orders to take command of the British army in North America. While this represented the highlight of his military career, Howe battled conflicting emotions. He yearned to lead armies into battle, yet hesitated to

Howe's Love of Leisure

Off the battlefield, William Howe established a reputation for enjoying the pleasures of life. As a result, contemporary satirists took advantage by penning poems mocking the military commander. According to Benson Bobrick's *Angel in the Whirlwind,* when in winter quarters at Philadelphia, Howe spent a great amount of time in the company of a beautiful woman named Mrs. Loring, causing one poet to write,

Sir William, he, snug as a flea
Lay all this time a-snoring;
Nor dream'd of harm, as he lay warm
In bed with Mrs. Loring.

Another poet took aim at Howe's high living while George Washington's soldiers faced cold and hunger at nearby Valley Forge.

Awake, awake, Sir Billy
There's forage in the plain.
Ah! leave your little filly,
And open the campaign.

march against his colonial brethren. He had even promised the people of Nottingham that, as their representative in Parliament, he would not accept a post against the colonies. Some prominent commanders, including Jeffrey Amherst, had declined promotions and others had resigned their military commissions rather than fight against the colonies.

Howe, though, accepted the challenge. He believed that with the friendly feelings that existed in the colonies toward his family, he could persuade the colonists to remain loyal to the king. He contended that few Americans openly favored rebellion and that most men and women only needed a reason to maintain their bonds with England. In explaining his decision to his Nottingham constituents, Howe mentioned that he could not refuse an order from his king to serve, especially in such tumultuous times.

The explanation failed to sway many people. One voter wrote Howe, "If you should resolve, at all events to go, I don't wish you may fall [in battle] as many do; but I cannot wish success to the undertaking."[11] Torn with conflicting emotions that boded ill for a man about to lead thousands of men into battle, Howe arrived in Boston on May 25, 1775.

The Battle of Bunker Hill

Howe had little time to reflect on circumstances, as the Americans had already gathered for battle near the Massachusetts capital. Instead of hastening to the battle area, though, Howe collected his forces as if he had all the time in the world. This meticulousness in preparation hurt Howe more than helped, since it handed the Americans more time to fortify their lines at the top of a hill overlooking Boston.

The British soldiers who stood at the base of Breed's Hill and gathered at nearby Bunker Hill looked, on June 17, 1775, splendid in their blazing red uniforms. With banners flying and flags snapping in the breeze, the units waited for the word from their commander to begin the ascent toward the American lines. Howe and his subordinate officers hoped—almost expected—that the Americans, many dressed in frontier garb or other civilian clothing instead of impressive uniforms, would panic at the sight of Europe's most vaunted military machine.

Howe erred in this assumption. As the British soldiers stepped in unison toward the top, drums beating a steady rhythm, American officers ordered their men to hold their fire until the British came within easy range. They then reminded their men to aim for the belt buckle and to focus their fire on British officers. The resulting slaughter shocked observers, and within minutes the remnants of the British assaulting force stumbled its way back down the hill, often stepping over or on the bodies of slain comrades.

Howe, refusing to believe the Americans would continue to stand up to the power of the British army, quickly or-

This engraving depicts the Battle of Bunker Hill, which took the lives of many soldiers.

dered a second attack. When this also met with disaster and more dead—some companies lost 90 percent of their men, and mangled bodies littered the slopes everywhere—some of Howe's subordinate officers urged him to retreat. Howe, correctly sensing that both his reputation and the honor of the British army rested on this initial battle against untested foes, regrouped the survivors and ordered a third attack. He told his men to toss away any unnecessary equipment so they could advance faster, then stepped to the front to lead one of the assaulting columns in a bayonet charge.

The subsequent maneuver produced similar grisly scenes, as American fire slowly reduced the British ranks as the soldiers marched upward. In some companies every officer had fallen, leaving only privates to carry the load. Others shouted, "Push on, push on" as they worked toward the top. Every one of Howe's aides, most standing at his side, fell in the assault, and so much blood blanketed the field that Howe's white leggings turned red.

With Howe in front of one of the columns, the British finally reached the summit and forced the Americans to fall back. Howe had saved Britain's honor and his military career, but the cost had been exorbitant. More than two hundred dead and over eight hundred wounded soldiers lay on the hill's slopes, almost half of the total number of troops used.

Another British officer, Henry Clinton, exclaimed afterward, "A dear bought victory, another such would have ruined us."[12]

Though pleased with carrying the day, Howe considered the price for what he called the "unhappy day"[13] too high. He regretted the loss of so many young soldiers and promising officers, and vowed that whenever possible, in the future he would avoid ordering frontal assaults such as had occurred in this fight.

Caution Leads to Defeat

Instead of pursuing the Americans, Howe remained in Boston. He wanted to give his men time to regroup, and he preferred to wait until reinforcements arrived, whenever that might be. Then with only two months of summer remaining, Howe set his men to constructing a garrison in which they would be able to wait out the winter.

By selecting winter quarters in Boston instead of mounting an expedition into the American countryside, Howe followed established military doctrine as practiced in Europe, where commanders typically waited for better spring weather to march against the enemy. However, by doing this, Howe again handed Washington more time to reorganize his men. The Continental army at this stage of the war was still largely untrained, ill supplied, and low on numbers. A bold attack during the winter of 1775–1776 might have so demoralized the Americans that the war could have been ended before

the Declaration of Independence had even been signed. While Washington's men huddled against the cold in nearby camps, Howe elected to wait out the winter in comparative luxury.

Indecision now hampered Howe. When he commanded a smaller force, Howe had been decisive when necessary, but now that the burden of commanding the entire British might in North America lay on his shoulders, Howe buckled. Before Bunker Hill, he had hoped that the simple appearance of the British army in battle formations would send the foes running, but when this failed to happen, Howe appeared confused. Instead of taking the initiative, Howe allowed events to control him.

Into the leadership vacuum created by Howe's lack of a plan stepped George Washington, desperate enough to take the first in a series of bold steps that would mark his command. For in March of 1776 Washington hurriedly placed cannon and two thousand men on Dorchester Heights overlooking Boston. Howe, still comfortable in Boston, received the news with incredulity, having been certain that emplacing artillery on those heights was a task beyond Washington's comparatively few, green troops. "My God!" he exclaimed. "These fellows have done more work in one night than I could make my army do in three months."[14]

Now completely exposed to deadly American artillery fire, on March 8 Howe asked Washington for an honorable evac-

Howe and his men board ships leaving Boston. The British evacuated Boston after a speedy American vitory.

uation. In return for a pledge not to attack his army as it left Boston, Howe promised that he would leave the city intact. Nine days later Howe and seventeen thousand British soldiers boarded ships and sailed to New York.

The speedy victory delighted the Americans. Abigail Adams, wife of a future president, wrote a friend, "The more I think of it, the more amazed I am that they should leave such a harbor, such fortifications, such intrenchments [*sic*], and that we should be in peaceable possession of a town which we expected would cost us a river of blood."[15]

The events leading to the evacuation of Boston affected Howe's subsequent moves over the next two years. No longer under the charge of a courageous leader, Britain now had a timid commander at the helm. Horrified at the bloody results of Bunker Hill, Howe moved cautiously about the American countryside, preferring to outmaneuver Washington rather than outfight him. As a result, he missed

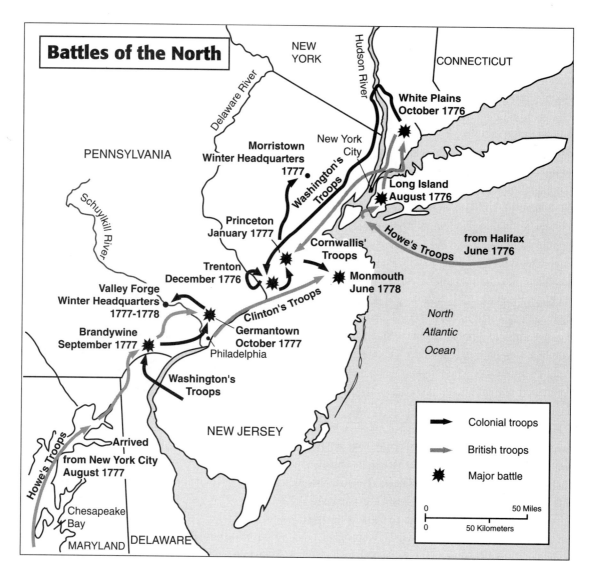

a handful of opportunities to inflict a deadly blow on his enemy.

Howe in New York

Howe landed in New York late in March but waited until August before advancing toward the east. When the two armies met near Brooklyn, on Long Island, Howe illustrated the military genius he had earlier promised by opting to strike against a weak American left flank instead of ordering a general assault, as he had done at Bunker Hill. The Americans lost almost one thousand dead and wounded, plus another eleven hundred taken captive against British losses of four hundred.

Again, though, Howe failed to take advantage of his win by pursuing Washington. He ordered Charles Cornwallis to halt at New Brunswick along the Delaware River, saying that his men needed rest from the battle just fought and assuring his fellow officer that the Americans would now offer to negotiate rather than continue challenging the British. Howe also felt that his main duty was to preserve his army rather than to take many casualties in repeated actions. He contended that a general had to rely on outmaneuvering his opponent rather than outfighting him, as if he and Washington commanded their respective forces on an immense chessboard.

The results were predictable. When Howe went into winter quarters at the Delaware River, he spared Washington to fight another day. A strong foray by Howe against the Americans might have ended the war right there, since Washington's forces were so weakened, but Howe selected rest and leisure over an arduous winter campaign.

Howe seemed to have risen above the level of his abilities. While a major leading troops up the Heights of Abraham, Howe showed ability and courage, but as commander in chief of the entire British army, he faced tasks for which he seemed ill suited. Some individuals who sparkle in secondary roles falter when given heavier responsibilities. Howe fell into that category.

Allan Maclean, one of Howe's subordinate officers, wrote a friend of Howe, "Brave he certainly is and would make a very good executive officer under another's command, but he is not by any means equal to Commander in Chief."[16]

Meanwhile, unlike his opponent, Washington exhibited enormous command skill. Refreshed with the reprieve from battle, Washington collected additional ammunition and brought up more food and other supplies, then after a brief period of reorganization, crossed the Delaware River in the dead of winter and launched his unexpected December 1776 blows against both Trenton and Princeton in New Jersey. The pair of victories breathed new hope into Washington's ranks and instilled a confidence with which they approached the fighting to come in 1777. Howe could have preempted both by his own bold move before settling into winter quarters.

The Battles of Brandywine and Germantown

Once the spring of 1777 arrived, Howe again moved slowly, still hoping to outmaneuver Washington and force him into peace talks. If he could not do that, Howe intended to seize Philadelphia, the American seat of government.

To check the British move to Philadelphia, Washington dug in along the Brandywine Creek. Howe sent two-thirds of his men around the American right flank, while the other one-third pinned down

Washington's forces with a diversionary attack against the middle. An attack in September forced Washington to fall back and left the door wide open to Philadelphia.

With a victory tucked under his arm, Howe assumed the fighting had ended for a time, but Washington had other ideas in mind. The American commander organized four columns of soldiers for an October 4 attack at Germantown. The initial charge threw British lines into disarray and caused troops to fall back. Howe, stunned that Washington could so quickly recover from Brandywine, went from group to group on the battlefield shouting, "I never saw you retreat before! It's only a scouting party!"[17] With this encouragement from their leaders and aided by a thick fog, the British succeeded in forging

through and breaking up resistance. Again, Washington had to pull back.

The twin victories opened the path to Philadelphia for Howe. As American political leaders fled, British infantry slowly approached and occupied the key city. Once more, Howe failed to follow through. Instead of pursuing the retreating Washington, who settled into 1777–1778 winter quarters at nearby Valley Forge, Howe called off military operations until the spring and focused on the pleasures offered by Philadelphia society. As one German officer stated, "Sir William liked to enjoy himself, so much

British forces defeat the Americans at the Battle of Germantown, paving the way for Howe's occupation of Philadelphia.

British revolutionary commander in chief, William Howe, shortly before his departure to England.

so that he sometimes forgot his duties as a commander."[18]

With his failure to finish Washington in 1777, Howe's detractors grew bolder in their condemnation of the British commander in chief. They blamed Howe for another general's loss of a crucial battle, and they charged Howe with leading his forces too leisurely at times that begged for bold, drastic action. One observer at the time wondered how "such an army, so well appointed, served by so large a train of artillery, and attended by so numerous a fleet, could fail of success against a divided people, destitute of Officers, Soldiers, Magazines [ammunition], fortified towns, ships of war, or any apparent resources."[19]

Return to England

Eager to defend his reputation, Howe asked permission to resign his command so he could return to England to answer his critics. He sailed for England on May 25, 1778, three years to the day since his arrival in North America. At an official inquiry into his conduct, he argued that he had been more aggressive in command than his critics claimed, that the loyalist forces in America were of little help, and that he lacked enough men to finish his task.

His accusers rebutted with a lengthy list of charges. According to them, Howe lacked a clear plan for defeating Washington, he allowed favorable feelings toward the Americans to affect his decisions, and he was too cautious. A lengthy investigation bogged down in politics, with Howe's supporters and opponents trading barbs and accusations. An inconclusive report from a military investigation board failed to settle the issue.

Despite the controversy, William Howe retained the respect of many Englishmen, both in and out of government. He continued to represent Nottingham in Parliament until 1780, when he lost in a reelection bid. He served in various military posts, mainly commanding different military districts inside England. After retiring from the army in 1803, he became the governor of Plymouth in 1805. He died there on July 12, 1814, at the age of eighty-five.

Chapter 3

Horatio Gates: Hero or Coward?

Each war produces an array of figures, some courageous, others timid, most who simply carry out their responsibilities and vanish into the pages of history. Horatio Gates fails to fit comfortably into any category. The leader gained adulation for his efforts at Saratoga, then received ridicule for his flight from Camden. History's judgment reflects the same tendency, as historians both praise and condemn the Revolutionary War leader, who excelled in the preliminaries of battle, such as logistics, training, and planning. Once the fighting started, however, his value tended to diminish.

Before the Revolution

Gates rose quickly through the ranks of the British military, mainly because, despite humble beginnings, he carried the backing of one of England's most powerful families. Born July 26, 1727, in Maldon, Essex, England, he was the son of Robert Gates, a tradesman, and Dorothea Gates,

who was housekeeper for the Duke of Leeds. The noble family enjoyed numerous influential connections in the British government and military, one of whom, politician Horace Walpole, became Horatio's godfather. Later the combined efforts of Walpole and the duke produced a commission in the army for Gates, a prize unheard of for a young man of his background. In 1749 Gates joined the British army as a lieutenant.

His initial assignment sent Gates to North America, where he served in Nova Scotia. Again, connections helped place him in a beneficial position. The lieutenant governor of Annapolis Royal, General Robert Monckton, befriended Gates, with whom he developed such close ties that Gates later named his only son after him. In 1754 he married Elizabeth Phillips, a member of an influential family in Nova Scotia enjoying considerable power back home. One year later, in the early days of the Seven Years' War, Gates joined General Braddock's army moving against the French at Fort Duquesne in present-day Pennsylvania and in Virginia.

Gates almost failed to survive his first day in combat. While gallantly leading his company of British soldiers, he was hit by a French musket ball. His men quickly formed a defensive line near the fallen officer, and while they directed a heavy volley of fire toward the enemy, a private, Francis Penfold, risked his life to drag Gates to safety barely before the French and their Indian allies reached him.

Some historians claim that Gates never forgot the incident. Later, when he commanded large numbers of soldiers for the Continental army in the Revolution, Gates established a reputation for treating his men with respect at a time when harsh discipline was the norm. Following the Revolution he even offered assistance to the financially strapped Penfold. "Come and rest your firelock in my chimney corner, and partake with me," he wrote Penfold, "while I have my savior Penfold shall not want."[20]

Gates recovered from his wounds sufficiently to join General Monckton in a successful 1761 expedition against the French

Washington leads General Braddock's army against French forces at Fort Duquesne in 1755.

in Martinique in the West Indies. Gates's efficient work helped bolster his reputation as a military commander and established him in the colonies as a good man to have around whenever danger developed.

Gates also gained valuable military experience and knowledge of the land during all this fighting. He fought over some of the same ground upon which he would later command troops against the British, and he observed the deadly frontier tactics employed by the French and Indians, especially their love for ambush-style strikes as opposed to fighting in the open in the European fashion. Most important, Gates learned how to handle the common soldier and Native allies.

Gates returned to England in 1762 to bring news of Monckton's victory over the French at Martinique. Though he enjoyed celebrity status for a time because of the colonial triumph and was promoted to major, Gates realized that little awaited him in the peacetime conditions. With the army reducing its ranks, Gates faced such an uncertain future that he resigned in 1765 to focus on business opportunities.

"Boston Dirt Will Be a Dollar a Bushell"

While in England, Gates continued a correspondence with George Washington, with whom he had served during Braddock's campaign. The American beguiled Gates with the benefits of living in the New World, where one did not have to rely on connections and nobility to be a

success but could instead fashion a career on talent. Gates eventually succumbed to Washington's arguments and moved to Virginia in 1772, where he purchased a plantation in western Virginia named Travellers' Rest. He easily mingled in society, holding the rank of lieutenant colonel in the colony's militia and sharing friendships with Washington and other Virginia leaders.

As the debate over unfair taxes and other British policies drove the colonies and Great Britain toward open conflict, Gates took an active role in favor of independence. When the war started in April 1775, he joined Washington's staff, where he employed his vast skills in administration and organization to help fashion an effective fighting force.

As brigadier general, Gates assumed command of the Continental forces near Boston. He took a novice army and, through constant drilling and training, turned them into a decent unit. Gates helped write the first set of regulations for Washington's army, established a reliable system for keeping records, and set up a program for recruiting new soldiers.

Possibly even more valuable was the advice he had for other generals. Some urged Washington to assume the offensive in an attempt to drive the British out of Boston, but Gates countered that the best course would be to wait outside the city, confine the enemy to Boston, and watch as British forces drained Britain's supplies and money. He wrote to an associ-

Gates is appointed to Washington's military staff in April 1775.

Gates in New York

Along with the promotion came a new command for Gates—that of the Northern Army. He took over at a difficult time, since the army was in disarray and losing ground to a determined British advance. Rebel leader John Adams wrote a friend, "Our Army at Crown Point [New York] is an object of wretchedness to fill a humane mind with horrour; disgraced, defeated, discontented, diseased, naked, undisciplined, eaten up with vermin; no clothes, no beds, blankets, no medicines; no victuals [food], but salt pork and flour."[22]

Gates himself realized that the most serious problems facing his men did not come from the enemy, but from within their own ranks. Lax discipline produced an ineffective fighting force; disease riddled the hapless men; a string of defeats demoralized the soldiers and caused numerous desertions. Gates faced the bleak prospect of commanding an army in shambles precisely at a time when General Sir Guy Carleton prepared to push south from Canada down Lake Champlain.

With little time to spare, Gates implemented his measures. He pulled his men back to Ticonderoga, farther away from Canada. Gates then attacked the deplorable medical conditions. He acquired medical supplies to battle smallpox and placed ill men in separate tents. Gates also ordered that each man receive an extra issue of rum, a move that may have had little medicinal value but certainly made him popular with his men.

ate, "Boston Dirt will be a Dollar a Bushell to the English Treasury. The Army, the Fleet, seventy Transports, and an infinity of Cutters etc. in constant pay."[21]

The tactic contributed to an American victory. When the British pulled out of Boston, on May 16, 1776, the Continental Congress rewarded Gates with a promotion to major general.

To remedy a food shortage so severe that many men subsisted on nothing but flour baked into thin cakes, Gates arranged for the delivery of cattle and a large amount of bread. In addition, he permitted local food dealers to sell directly to the men. Soon, soldiers feasted on vegetables, cheese, sugar, and wine. Within a short time, morale soared.

At the same time Gates began building a fleet of ships to counter Carleton and appointed Benedict Arnold to command the fleet. Carleton hoped to move speedily down into New York, cut off New England from the other colonies, and bring the war's end near, but following a naval encounter against Arnold on October 11, 1776, off Valcour Island in Lake Champlain, the British halted their advance and returned to Canada.

This delay meant that the next spring British general John Burgoyne would start from distant Canada instead of from a more advantageous position in northern New York. It also handed Gates and other Continental officers additional time to prepare for that invasion. This delay made the colonial triumph at Saratoga possible.

Disaster at Ticonderoga

Gates returned to New York in the spring of 1777 after spending the winter in Philadelphia. Everyone knew that Gen-

The Americans fail in their attempt to secure the fort from Burgoyne in the Battle of Ticonderoga.

eral Burgoyne's British forces would make another attempt to plunge from Canada deep into New York and sever present-day New England from the rest of the colonies. It was clear, as well, that much of the early fighting would occur near Fort Ticonderoga. Another general, Philip Schuyler, took command at the strong point and waited for his foe to arrive.

Ticonderoga was a star-shaped fort bristling with armament. Almost 150 cannon guarded the approaches, a potent arsenal that made anyone think twice before assaulting the location. Overlooking Fort Ticonderoga to the immediate west was Sugar Loaf Hill, but neither Schuyler nor Gates thought that Burgoyne could maneuver cannon up Sugar Loaf's steep eight-hundred-foot slopes. Thus they failed to occupy this important strategic position. In March 1777, when Burgoyne's men managed to reach the top of Sugar Loaf, nothing prevented them from securing cannon at the crest. Faced with the prospect of a lethal volume of enemy fire from above, Schuyler had no choice but to remove his men from the fort

The loss of Ticonderoga stunned the Americans. Many claimed that a traitorous act must have led to the fort's fall and demanded the removal of either Schuyler or Gates. John Adams stated that "I believe we shall never hold a post until we shoot a general."[23]

As Gates had not been present at Ticonderoga and Schuyler had, the latter was removed shortly after the loss. Gates returned to the region with his reputation sullied, but intact. He understood, however, that should Burgoyne crash through his lines and threaten lower New York, his military career would quickly end.

The Road to Saratoga

At Ticonderoga, Gates had exhibited both his talents and his shortcomings. His ability to restore morale and locate supplies seemed unrivaled, but his skill on the battlefield had not been tested. Instead, a grave strategic error had been committed. Now Gates knew that Burgoyne would try to achieve victory before winter, but rather than make a bold preemptive strike, he fell back on the cautious approach he knew so well from his earlier war experiences: digging in and waiting for his enemy to appear.

Benedict Arnold and Thaddeus Kosciuszko, a general from Poland with a background in engineering, scouted the region for the most advantageous spot from which to oppose Burgoyne. They settled on Bemis Heights, a well-protected plot of land lying between steep cliffs and the Hudson River. To pass through the area, Burgoyne would have to advance directly across the dwelling of a local resident, Freeman's Farm. Gates implemented a plan that placed sharpshooters under Colonel Daniel Morgan and Lieutenant Colonel Henry Dearborn to the left, militia on the right, and New England's best soldiers in the middle under Gates's personal command. It was September 19, 1777.

The stage had been set for the first of two crucial clashes that the Battle of Saratoga comprises: Freeman's Farm and Bemis Heights. After the smoke cleared, the Continental army had turned back Burgoyne and handed Washington a badly needed victory.

The Battle of Freeman's Farm

Burgoyne's men, with brilliant red uniforms and bayonets flashing in the sun, were plainly visible as they advanced toward Freeman's Farm, a clearing 350 yards long consisting of fifteen to twenty acres of land surrounding a log home. Rather than attacking or relying on the frontier tactics of fighting from behind trees and ambushes that had so confused

Britain in previous encounters, however, Gates confined his soldiers to hastily erected defensive fortifications.

Burgoyne's force advanced in three columns. One group, mainly Hessian soldiers from Germany, moved along a river road, intent on attacking the American right flank. A mixture of British, Americans loyal to the king, and Native Americans under General Simon Fraser swung around the American left edge to bring fire along the entire Continental line, while Burgoyne commanded the forces assaulting the middle. Initially, Gates

Freeman's Farm, pictured here, was the site of a bloody battle on September 19, 1777.

passed up the chance to attack any of the British units before all were in place, despite the urging of Benedict Arnold, his second in command.

Because of Arnold's persistence, however, Gates finally dispatched the sharpshooters under Morgan and Dearborn to bring fire on the column approaching the left flank. As Burgoyne's men stepped out of the woods in the vicinity of Freeman's Farm, a deadly volley stopped them in their tracks.

For the rest of the day, fighting enveloped the open area at Freeman's Farm, but when darkness fell, Burgoyne's men held the open land and Gates had pulled his troops back to his fortifications.

By holding the clearing at Freeman's Farm, Burgoyne had technically won the day, but he had paid an exorbitant price. American sharpshooters in trees had killed most of the British officers, severely weakening Burgoyne's army. One officer who survived, Lieutenant Thomas Anbury, wrote to a friend, "I am fearful the advantage resulting from this hard-fought battle will rest on that of the Americans, our army being so weakened by this engagement as not to be of sufficient strength to venture forth and improve the victory, which may, in the end, put a stop to our intended expedition."[24]

Anbury's perceptive statement adequately summarized the day's battle. The Americans lost 65 men killed, 218 wounded, and 36 missing. Burgoyne, on the other hand, read over the reports of his losses with dismay—600 killed, wounded, or captured.

The two sides settled into their respective camps to recuperate from the battle. Gates sent raiding parties out most nights to harass the British, but he continued on a collision course with Benedict Arnold, whom he relieved of command after an angry confrontation.

Burgoyne had intended to remain in his position until help arrived from Sir Henry Clinton. Upon learning that additional reinforcements would not be arriving, however, Burgoyne decided to attack the Americans quickly, hoping to avoid a humiliating wintertime retreat back into Canada.

The Battle of Bemis Heights

Seeing Burgoyne's troops were making no moves to retreat, Gates prepared for another assault by the British. "Perhaps his despair may dictate to [Burgoyne] to risque all upon one throw,"[25] Gates wrote to a friend, so he formulated a three-pronged counterattack should the enemy make a move.

On October 4, Burgoyne selected fifteen hundred of his best troops and led them in a bayonet charge against the Americans at Bemis Heights, a few miles south of Freeman's Farm. American sharpshooters halted the charge in its tracks, and, in the middle of the fighting, Arnold suddenly appeared on his horse, rallying the men to further effort. Although relieved of command in September, Arnold

This 1777 engraving depicts the British encampment at Saratoga, New York.

could not stand idle while the men he still regarded as his troops did nothing.

Arnold rode everywhere, shouting words of encouragement and directing the men toward a vital portion of Burgoyne's line. When the Americans overran that section, Burgoyne's line collapsed and forced him to pull away from the battlefield, with a retreat to Canada now his only option. A speedy move placed American forces at Burgoyne's rear, blocking his retreat. With supplies running low and desertions decimating his ranks, Burgoyne chose to surrender. Near the village of Saratoga, on October 17, 1777, he and Gates finalized the terms.

The American victory that culminated at Saratoga proved decisive in the war. Not only had the colonists captured a large army, but they placed doubts in the minds of British military comman-

ders that the Americans could be defeated. In addition, the French, bitter enemies of the English, having seen evidence that the Americans could mount an effective fight, declared war on Great Britain. John Adams, who had been in Paris attempting to persuade France to send military assistance, wrote that "General Gates was the ablest negotiator you ever had in Europe."[26]

Americans hailed Gates as a hero for the triumph at Saratoga, even though many observers credited Arnold, who had appeared on the field of combat, exhorting the men to victory, while Gates had remained at his headquarters almost three miles away. Although Gates said he had had to stay close to headquarters to receive reports from his commanders, some suggested that he had avoided the fight out of cowardice. It would not be the last time Gates was accused of lacking courage.

Catastrophe at Camden

For some time, Gates had been asking to be relieved so he could return home for a much-needed rest. The Continental Congress granted his wish in 1779, but his respite was to last less than one year. After the stinging rebuke at Saratoga, British military leaders switched the focus of their operations to the southern states, and on May 12, 1780, American general Benjamin Lincoln surrendered fifty-five hundred soldiers after a defeat at Charleston, South Carolina.

In desperation, the Continental Congress called Gates out of his brief retirement, placed him in command of the Southern Department, tasked with reversing the situation in South Carolina. The man who received credit for Saratoga headed south with high expectations, but with the warning of neighbor Charles Lee ringing in his ears: "Take care lest your Northern laurels turn to Southern willows."[27]

Gates arrived in North Carolina on July 25, 1780, only to discover an army of hungry, ill-prepared men, demoralized from repeated defeats. He decided to attack the British before more desertions depleted his ranks.

Within two days of his arrival, Gates had his men marching toward a British stronghold at Camden, South Carolina, and on August 16 arrayed those troops in battle formations for an assault against Cornwallis. The attack, which pitted untrained, weary militia against veteran soldiers, was doomed before it started. Observing the American movements through field glasses, British general Charles Cornwallis quickly discovered a weakness—the American left side advanced hesitantly, almost as though the men did not want to move. He immediately ordered a bayonet charge against that side of the line, which quickly dissolved in panic. With the left side collapsed, the American center had to pull back to avoid being trapped.

Gates tried desperately to halt the retreat, but then rather than remain on the battlefield, he turned to the rear and rode away. Amazingly, the commander did not stop until three and one-half days later, by which time he had traveled a distance of 180 miles.

Camden proved to be a costly defeat for the Americans and for Gates. The road to North Carolina and Virginia lay wide open, and Gates received stinging criticism for what many called his cowardly flight. He answered that he was only trying to reach friendly territory where he could reorganize the men, but doubters wondered why he selected a spot so far from the fighting. Political leader Alexander Hamilton asked, "Was there ever an instance of a General running away as Gates has done from his whole army?"[28] The

Continental Congress removed Gates from command in October 1780 and ordered an inquiry into the debacle.

Final Years

Gates retired in shame to Travellers' Rest, but labored for two years to clear his name. When Congress dropped an inquiry in 1782 without bringing charges, he felt exonerated and rejoined the military. The next year Gates returned to Virginia to Elizabeth, who was critically ill. After the death of his wife, Gates lived quietly on the plantation until July 1786, when he married again. The second Mrs. Gates was a wealthy widow, the former Mary Vallance. Four years later he sold Travellers' Rest, freed his slaves, and moved to New York where he served in the state legislature.

Gates died on April 10, 1806, in New York City, still the subject of controversy. His defenders argued that Gates helped win the war with his command at Saratoga, while his detractors stated that Benedict Arnold had more to do with the victory than Gates. Critics also pointed to his poor record in the South as proof that the man lacked the ability to lead soldiers in battle.

Gates remains an enigma to this day. Was he an able patriot who aided the American cause, or was he an incom-

Despite Gates's largely illustrious military career, he remains a subject of controversy due to his retreat at Camden.

petent field officer whose mistakes and cowardice contributed to costly defeat? It appears in retrospect that, like many men, Gates could show flashes of brilliance on some occasions, and instances of ineptness on others. Unfortunately for him, his unaccountable flight from Camden overshadows his other, more significant, contributions.

Chapter 4

John Burgoyne: The Dashing General

General John Burgoyne may have been the most complex commanding officer to fight in the American Revolution. He was a serious student of military history who loved reading and writing plays. His soldiers slept on the ground and endured the miseries of war while Burgoyne lived in comparative luxury, yet he was beloved by his troops. The British king heralded his accomplishments early in the war, then removed him from command later in the conflict. The dashing John Burgoyne cut a handsome figure, one more fit for the stage than the battlefield.

Early Life

John Burgoyne was born on February 2, 1722, in Hackney, Middlesex, England, to a prominent family. King Charles I had granted a baroncy to the family, and in 1387 the Burgoyne family had received extensive land from the government. His mother was the daughter of an important merchant, while the man who was most likely Burgoyne's father, Captain John Burgoyne, lost most of the family wealth at the gambling tables. Rumors circulated in British society that someone else had fathered young John Burgoyne, most likely a nobleman, a close adviser to Queen Anne.

Burgoyne was educated at the Westminster School, an institution catering to the upper class. While there he befriended the son of the Earl of Derby, a powerful individual with connections in the government and military. On one of the frequent visits to his friend's estate, Burgoyne met and fell in love with his schoolmate's sister, Lady Charlotte Stanley. Despite opposition from the Earl of Derby, who hesitated to let his daughter marry a future soldier, Burgoyne and Lady Charlotte married in 1743. The Earl of Derby promptly cut the couple off from family money, although he at least bestowed a large enough dowry on the couple to enable Burgoyne to leave

British general John Burgoyne was beloved by his troops.

the civilian world and join the military as a captain in the Thirteenth Dragoons, a cavalry outfit.

Military service in the eighteenth century differed from today's in that officers were not paid unless war or other serious matters required their active participation. Once the threat vanished, officers were expected to return to their civilian occupations. For Burgoyne, who enjoyed no steady income outside the military and received little help from either his or his wife's family, this meant frequent lapses into debt. In 1751, pursued by creditors, Burgoyne and wife fled to France.

The couple lived on the Continent for five years, where Burgoyne indulged his taste for the arts. A skilled writer himself, Burgoyne associated with the most talented stars of the French artistic community and studied French culture. This was the beginning of a lifelong love affair with the arts, particularly writing for the stage.

After the five-year period ended, the Burgoynes returned to England. Most likely the Earl of Derby, after ending the quarrel with his son-in-law, had paid off the couple's debts. With relations between Britain and France deteriorating and the threat of war looming, Burgoyne rejoined the military in 1756. Three years later the king asked Burgoyne to raise one of the two new regiments of light cavalry, the Sixteenth Light Dragoons.

Attracting Attention

Burgoyne's military endeavors in the 1750s and 1760s gained the notice of his superiors. Along with the patronage of important people he always seemed to cultivate, Burgoyne rapidly rose to higher command.

Even so, like many successful people, Burgoyne was the target of vicious verbal attacks by those who resented his triumphs. Critics pictured Burgoyne as an arrogant man who let personal pursuits interfere with his military duties. They castigated him as a playboy who preferred to gamble, consort with beautiful women, and spend hours discussing the arts and academic topics with fellow intellectuals. One critic, noted writer Horace Walpole, labeled Burgoyne "General Swagger" for the way he strutted about London as if he were the most important individual in the land.

His rivals were not entirely incorrect in their condemnations. The tall, handsome Burgoyne did enjoy books and writing, and he seemed to attract attention from most women who encountered him. In North American military campaigns, he even traveled with his own retinue of associates and ate with fine silver and off exquisite tablecloths.

However, Burgoyne had a serious professional side. He disagreed with most of the military authorities of his day in his approach to disciplining the troops. Rather than employ harsh measures—British soldiers were often subject to whippings—Burgoyne preferred to treat the men under his command with respect. The educated Burgoyne, the man who loved the arts and believed that reason could triumph over brutality, warned his officers, "There are two systems which divide the disciplinarians: the one [from the harsh German system] is that of training men like spaniels, by the stick; the other, after the French, of substituting the point of honor in the place of severity. I apprehend [promote] a just medium between the two extremes."[29] Consequently, Burgoyne gained the deep affection of his men, who called him Gentleman Johnny.

The Seven Years' War, called the French and Indian War in North America, handed Burgoyne an opportunity to prove his abilities. He became a firm advocate of the full capabilities of cavalry—as a means of rapid advancement and quick thrusts. He constantly drilled his men so they could execute orders in unison, and he dressed them in impressive uniforms to develop a feeling of pride and cohesiveness. Burgoyne so excelled in raids against coastal towns in France that he earned a promotion to lieutenant colonel, and reveled in hearing others depict his unit as "Burgoyne's Light Horse."

Politician in Parliament

Following the war, Burgoyne returned to England in hopes that he could promote his military career by developing important contacts in the political realm. In a bitterly contested 1768 election campaign, which saw Burgoyne visit the polling place with an armed guard and carrying a loaded pistol in each hand, he won a seat in Parliament that he held for the rest of his life.

Burgoyne's strategy of using a political life to further his military ambitions worked. In 1769 he was appointed governor of Fort William in North America, a post that normally went to officers higher in rank than Burgoyne, and three years later he was promoted to major general and posted to England.

Burgoyne enjoyed London life. As a lover of the arts, he associated with writers and actors, including the renowned Shakespearean actor, David Garrick. In 1774 he authored a play titled *Maid of the*

British troops attack French-occupied Quebec during the Seven Years' War.

Oaks, a biting examination of the role of class in British society.

During the heated pre–Revolutionary War years, Burgoyne believed the British government was too lenient on the colonies. In Parliament he advocated continued taxing, and in an April 1774 speech against repealing taxes he said, "I look upon America to be our child, which I think we have already spoiled by too much indulgence."[30]

He was about to become very familiar with that child. Events heated to the breaking point shortly after Burgoyne's speech in Parliament, and once more the officer found himself heading to battle, this time in North America.

To the Revolution

In February 1775 Burgoyne crossed the Atlantic Ocean in the company of two other top commanders, General Sir William Howe and General, later Sir, Henry Clinton. Now that open fighting had started in the colonies, the officers carried orders to assist a colleague, General Thomas Gage, in dispersing the rebels in the Boston area. Burgoyne observed the action at Breed's Hill and concluded that many of his peers were underestimating the Americans.

Burgoyne was assigned the second in command to Major General Guy Carleton, who commanded the forces about to move south from Canada into upper New York for the 1776 campaign against the Continental army. Instead of studying the North American terrain, the colonial fashion of warfare, and the political moods of the region, Burgoyne spent more time writing letters to prominent supporters in England or to fellow officers to gain the support of influential individuals. The brash Burgoyne criticized his superiors and condemned those he considered rivals for power.

When the 1776 campaign ended, aiming to further promote himself to the men who made the decisions on future military strategy, Burgoyne returned to England. There be presented his plan for a four-pronged attack in North America which, he argued, could bring victory in 1777. King George III personally approved the plan, whereupon Burgoyne prepared to head back to North America and glory.

In the campaign he had designed, Burgoyne showed both abilities and faults. He correctly understood that the war in America did not simply pit foe against foe on the battlefield, but was a contest of ideas—colonial freedom versus the king's authority. He knew that he had to win the minds of the people as well as triumph on the battlefield, thus his campaigns typically included written proclamations—many penned by himself—to convince the

A meeting of two worlds: Canadian Native Americans encounter British soldiers led by Burgoyne.

colonials that they should remain loyal to the king. Burgoyne relied on three military tools to scare his opponents—cannon on a vast scale, cavalry to strike quickly, and most important, Native American fighters, which the colonials feared above all.

He exhibited failings as well. For example, he erred in assuming that the only strength of the colonial militia was in delaying actions. Above all, he relied too much on bayonet charges to frighten the enemy. He believed that anyone could fire a rifle, but only the bravest would charge across a field, bayonet at the ready, to kill their foe. He expected that any such attack would demoralize what he considered to be the untrained, unprofessional military assembled by the colonials.

Burgoyne's 1777 Campaign Begins

Burgoyne led his forces from St. Johns in Canada on June 12, 1777. Seven thousand regular soldiers, half from the British army and half paid German soldiers, led the way, followed by 600 artillerymen transporting 138 cannon. Bringing up the rear were 650 Canadian volunteers and 500 Native Americans, fewer than Burgoyne had hoped for. Intending to return from the expedition to glory and honor, he issued the order that there would be no retreat.

Burgoyne's vanity further prodded him to issue a proclamation to the Americans urging them to lay down their arms. He believed that his talent as a writer might overcome their objections and

Untimely Interruption

Burgoyne traveled to the American colonies to help restore order for the king, but he also found time to promote his intellectual interests. Before the Battle of Bunker Hill Burgoyne wrote a small play titled *The Siege of Boston,* in which he used his cutting wit to present his views of the current situation. The audience failed to see the finish of the January 8, 1776, performance in Charleston, Massachusetts, however. The actor portraying Washington had just entered the stage when a British sergeant burst into the theater with the news that the Americans had attacked Bunker Hill. At first the audience assumed the sergeant was another actor in the play, but they quickly learned otherwise when every military officer in the theater rushed from the room.

convince the Americans their cause was in error, but only derisive laughter greeted the pompous proclamation:

> The domestic, the industrious, the infirm, and even the timid inhabitants, I am desirous to protect, provided they remain quietly at their houses; that they do not suffer their cattle to be removed, nor their corn or forage to be secreted or destroyed; that they do not break up their bridges or roads; nor by any other act, directly or indirectly, endeavor to obstruct the operations of the King's troops, or supply or assist those of the enemy. Every species of provision brought to my camp, will be paid for at an equitable rate, and in solid coin.[31]

Burgoyne then added an ominous threat. Although he had ordered his Native allies to engage in no bloodshed outside the battle—no colonists slaughtered, no women and children scalped—he wrote as follows to the Americans: "I have but to give stretch to the Indian forces under my direction, and they amount to thousands, to overtake the hardened enemies of Great Britain."[32] The attempt at intimidation only served to rouse more anger and opposition among the Americans.

Success Is Followed by Setbacks

The campaign started with a resounding success for Burgoyne. On July 1 he landed his forces north of Fort Ticonderoga, the fortress that had been the scene of so many assaults during the French and Indian War. Burgoyne spotted the nearby hill named Sugar Loaf, which the Americans had judged to be an insurmountable obstacle, and ordered his engineers to hack out a road to the top. If he could place cannon at the crest, Burgoyne knew the Americans in the fort below would be helpless against his fire. Within one day his engineers had finished their task. The bombardment began and the Americans swiftly abandoned Fort Ticonderoga.

The quick victory deluded Burgoyne and the British into thinking they faced poorly trained opponents, and that the Revolution was all but over. People in England praised Burgoyne's name, church bells rang in triumph, and King George III shouted to his wife, "I've beat them! Beat all the Americans!"[33]

Burgoyne now made a decision that would have immense repercussions on his campaign. The next step in the plan the king had approved called for Burgoyne to arrive near Albany and meet with General Howe. Not wanting to appear to be in retreat by taking an indirect route through British-controlled territory, Burgoyne chose to try to move his thousands of troops on a straight-line path through dense forests.

The thickly wooded terrain proved almost impassable, however, with branches and trees blocking the narrow, hardly visible paths. Burgoyne's engineers cleared the primitive roads and built bridges, but one thousand American axmen felled innumerable trees in his way and shoved boulders down slopes to block the advance. Instead of arriving at his destination in a week, Burgoyne required three weeks to move twenty-three miles, only to find that General Howe was not heading north to meet him, but was instead retiring to Philadelphia.

Two setbacks then occurred in swift fashion. In dire need of supplies, Burgoyne dispatched 650 men into the Connecticut Valley with orders to obtain all the horses and supplies they could find, by any means. When the Native Americans accompanying this group took the opportunity to settle old scores with the American settlers, however, most fled their farms and took their livestock along.

Thus a valuable supply of food was denied Burgoyne.

The second setback occurred only six days later, when the troops led by another British general in the nearby Mohawk Valley fell to superior American forces in brutal hand-to-hand combat. Contrary to normal practice of the time, Burgoyne did not order a general retreat following news of this second disaster, for he would not consider implementing such a blow to his honor.

Lacking supplies from the immediate region, Burgoyne halted his forces for a month while badly needed food and ammunition were brought from Canada. During this time, the Americans were able to bring up supplies and to construct sturdy defenses at Bemis Heights along the Hudson River in preparation for Burgoyne's advance. By September 9, more than seven thousand Americans manned these defenses and waited for Burgoyne to cross over the Hudson, a necessary move if he were to head to Albany. Four days later Burgoyne began the river crossing, ensuring that battle lay only days ahead.

The Battle of Freeman's Farm

The first of two encounters that comprise what is now called the Battle of Saratoga unfolded on September 19, when three columns of British soldiers advanced through the forests near the clearing called Freeman's Farm. A left wing under Major General Baron Friedrich von Riedesel headed along a road following

Burgoyne's newly assimilated Native American forces attack the fort in the Battle of Ticonderoga.

the Hudson River, while the middle force advanced through the forests under Burgoyne's command, protected on the right by men under General Simon Fraser.

The Americans were waiting for them to attack. During the fighting, General Benedict Arnold spotted a gap between Fraser and Burgoyne near Freeman's Farm. He quickly poured in soldiers, and for hours men clubbed, bayoneted, and shot each other as the fighting swerved back and forth. First the Americans appeared to have the advantage, then the British; cannon were captured, lost, and recaptured. One British regiment suffered 80 percent casualties.

Riedesel saved the day for the British. Without waiting for orders from Burgoyne, the German officer organized a relief regiment and led it to the top of a hill, from which point he could see British soldiers battling for their lives. Riedesel immediately swooped down the hill to crash into the unsuspecting Americans, who eventually fell back. At the end of the day, Burgoyne still controlled the battlefield, but the victory came at a heavy price: more than six hundred casualties.

Despite his losses, Burgoyne had planned to mount a second attack, for the Americans also had suffered heavy casualties, and he was expecting reinforcements from his own superior, General Sir Henry Clinton. The Americans took advantage of the lull not only to bring in supplies, but also harass the British. Sharpshooters climbed trees and patiently waited for a British officer to walk carelessly about camp or raise his head above a wall. Burgoyne later wrote that "not a night passed without firing, and sometimes concerted attacks, at our advanced pickets [outposts]. It was the plan of the enemy to harass the army by constant alarms and their superiority in number enabled them to attempt it without fatigue to themselves."[34]

As the days stretched on, Burgoyne found himself in a quandary. He had received no further word from Clinton, but he could not wait much longer for help to arrive. Each day, more men fell to sharpshooters and disease, or deserted their posts. With supplies running perilously low, Burgoyne concluded that he would have to act. To retreat was unacceptable, and so, after consulting with his top advisers, Burgoyne opted to charge the American positions.

The Battle of Bemis Heights

On October 7, British soldiers again advanced in three columns. The army moved to a clearing, then stopped along a one thousand-yard line to rest, allowing the Americans, under Gates, to slip through the woods and launch surprise attacks against either end of the line of troops. American sharpshooters and militia hit both flanks with such fury that the British fell back, exposing the forces in the middle. Bloody fighting swiftly engulfed the middle of the line, where British soldiers gallantly battled to hold their position, but the American superiority in numbers proved too much. When General Fraser, who had been a beacon of courage for his men, fell with a mortal wound, the British soldiers fled in panic. Benedict Arnold then won the day by leading charges through the crumbling British resistance and successfully attacking two of the strongholds the British had built while waiting for Clinton.

With his forces in disarray and in danger of being surrounded, Burgoyne had no choice but to retreat toward Canada. Along the route, sharpshooters again inflicted casualties, while American settlers felled trees to slow the pullback. More than twenty thousand Americans collected as Burgoyne fell back until the time came when he could no longer hope to elude his pursuers.

It was then that Burgoyne chose to negotiate surrender terms. Near the village

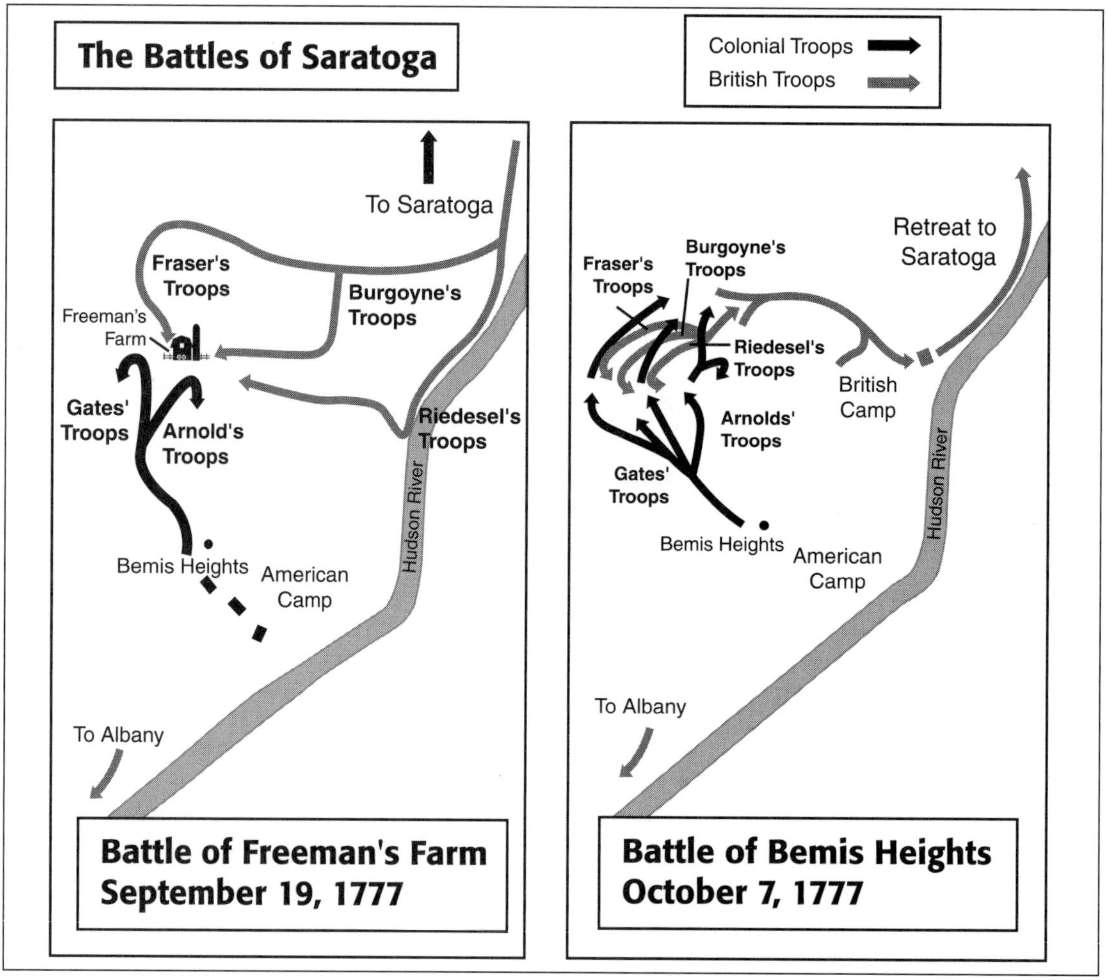

The Battles of Saratoga

Colonial Troops
British Troops

Battle of Freeman's Farm
September 19, 1777

To Saratoga
Fraser's Troops
Burgoyne's Troops
Freeman's Farm
Gates' Troops
Arnold's Troops
Riedesel's Troops
Hudson River
Bemis Heights
American Camp
To Albany

Battle of Bemis Heights
October 7, 1777

Fraser's Troops
Burgoyne's Troops
Retreat to Saratoga
Riedesel's Troops
British Camp
Arnolds' Troops
Gates' Troops
Hudson River
Bemis Heights
American Camp
To Albany

Generals Gates (center) and Burgoyne (left of center) negotiate terms of the British surrender on October 17, 1777.

of Saratoga, on October 17, 1777, he and Gates finalized the terms of surrender. As was traditional in European warfare, Burgoyne offered his sword to General Gates and said, "General, the caprice of war has made me your prisoner." The American refused to accept, however, and replied, "You will always find me ready to testify that it was not brought about through any fault of your excellency."[35] Burgoyne was able to lead his defeated ranks to Boston, where they boarded ships bound for England with the promise that they would never again be used to fight in America.

Final Years

Back in England, Burgoyne attempted to clear his reputation. He asked the British government to conduct an inquiry, but the panel's inconclusive report irritated Burgoyne. When he angrily offered to resign his military posts, the British govern-

ment surprised the general by accepting. Burgoyne found himself without a military career.

Fortunately, he had the arts to occupy his time. He resumed the writing of plays, and some critics called his comedy, *The Heiress,* the best of its day. For a time he rejoined the army as commander in chief in Ireland after a new government was formed, but when it fell Burgoyne was once again replaced.

On August 3, 1792, after years of arduous campaigning in some of the world's most primitive regions, Burgoyne died in London at the age of seventy. Perhaps the strain of Saratoga also proved too much for a man who took pride in name and reputation.

Chapter 5

John Paul Jones: Hero of the Seas

Most of the military successes and triumphs of the American Revolution occurred on land, where infantry, cavalry, and cannon dominated. At the same time, however, battles raged at sea, though with much less frequency. Of the handful of commanders to serve in either the British or American navies, one man emerges as the most influential. John Paul Jones not only carried the day in stirring sea actions, but he breathed life into the infant Continental navy, the forerunner to today's mighty United States Navy.

A Life by the Sea

John Paul, who later added the name Jones, was born in Kirkcudbrightshire, Scotland, on July 6, 1747. Both parents, John Paul Sr. and Jean MacDuff, worked for a wealthy neighboring landowner. His father served as the gardener to the estate of William Craik, while his mother worked as a housekeeper in Craik's manor. As part of their arrangement,

Craik built for the couple a stone cottage near the shore in which they could live.

They quickly filled the house with children. Son William, born in 1738, eventually moved to Fredericksburg, Virginia. Two daughters then followed before a second son, John Paul, was born. After him came two children who died as infants, and another daughter.

The family never went hungry, for as a gardener, John Paul Sr. enjoyed the rights to all the milk and vegetables they could consume, and living near the sea provided ample amounts of fish. The Pauls belonged to the local Presbyterian church and sent their sons to its school, but as an adult, Paul was never a churchgoer.

Little is known of Paul's life as a youngster. He had minimal formal schooling, but living near the sea he developed an interest in ships and seafaring. Whenever Paul could, he headed for the shore to talk to sailors and inspect ships, and many times as a youth he pretended to be a great captain in battle, standing a short distance from his playmates and barking orders as if they were under attack.

In 1761, at the age of thirteen, Paul left home to begin his apprenticeship as a ship's boy to a neighboring shipowner named John Younger. For the next seven years, according to his contract, he would serve Mr. Younger, at the end of which time he would be free to act on his own. John Paul stepped aboard a fishing vessel that took him to Whitehaven, in the north of England, where he caught a glimpse of the first ship in which he would serve—the brig *Friendship* under the command of Robert Benson.

A Tumultuous Rise to Command

For the next three years the *Friendship* shipped products, such as rum and sugar, to and from Scotland and Fredericksburg, Virginia. In 1764 John Younger fell on hard financial times, which forced him to release Paul from his seven-year contract. Paul immediately stepped into jobs on slave ships, including being the chief mate for the slaver *Two Friends* out of Jamaica, but he detested shipping human cargo to

This engraving of an eighteenth-century sailing ship is much like the one the young John Paul Jones served on as an apprentice.

the New World. He called the sordid business the "abominable trade."[36]

Paul booked a passage on another ship headed for England, the *John*. During the crossing, both the ship's captain and its chief mate died at sea. Since no one else knew how to navigate, Paul took over as the most experienced seaman and safely piloted the ship across the Atlantic to Scotland. For this feat, the owners handed him command of the ship for her next voyage.

The five-feet, five-inch Paul proved to be a hard captain. He battled a temper most of his life, and he rarely allowed personal considerations to complicate the business side of seafaring. He had reason to be serious, for the commander of a small ship had to do most of the navigating jobs as well as maintain order among the crew. Though still in his twenties, he handled the situation with firmness. The top benefit was that Paul, existing in a situation that demanded he act boldly and decisively, learned more at sea than most officers learned in three years of schooling.

Paul's first two voyages on the *John* took him back to Jamaica, and during the second trip he flogged the ship's carpenter, Mungo Maxwell, for breaking rules. Mungo

filed a formal complaint against Paul, which a court of inquiry promptly tossed out. Yet when Mungo died soon afterward, aboard a different ship, the carpenter's father complained to an English court that his son "was most unmercifully, by the said John Paul, with a great cudgel or batton, bled, bruized and wounded

This painting depicts a famous incident in which Captain Jones threatens the John's *carpenter, whose death he was arrested for.*

upon his back and other parts of his body, and of which wounds and bruizes he soon afterward died on board the *Barcelona Packet* of London."[37]

Arrested for murder upon his return to Scotland, Paul secured his release by promising to obtain information clearing his name. This he did, by traveling to the West Indies and transcribing the testimony of witnesses that Mungo was in good health when he left the *John.*

In 1773, while in command of another ship, *Betsy,* off the island of Tobago in the West Indies, Paul ran his sword through a mutinous sailor. On the advice of friends who feared that the victim's family might take matters into their own hands, Paul fled back to Fredericksburg. In America, to shield his identity, he added the surname Jones to his name. He arrived at an opportune moment, for the infant nation sought sailors and officers to man its fledgling fleet.

Jones Joins the Revolution

With the opening of conflict against the British, the Continental Congress formed a navy and ordered the conversion of a handful of merchant vessels to gunships. Jones traveled to Philadelphia to offer his services, claiming that he hoped to contribute to the cause of freedom and to halt tyranny, but he sought fame just as much. On December 7, 1775, he received a commission as a lieutenant in the Continental navy and was assigned to the *Alfred,* a thirty-gun frigate.

Jones gained notoriety the next year as commander of the frigate *Providence.* Sailing up and down the Atlantic coast, Jones attacked fisheries in Nova Scotia as well as British ships, capturing eight vessels and destroying eight others in less than two months. By the end of October, Jones had to cancel the expedition when he ran short of crew members—most of the *Providence* crew had to be detached to man the ships he had seized.

He continued to terrorize British shipping as captain of his old ship, the *Alfred.* His main prize was to seize a huge transport bulging with winter uniforms and other equipment intended for the British army. By the end of the year, Jones had been responsible for capturing or destroying twenty-two ships, including one that carried sixteen guns.

The Continental navy altered its strategy in 1777. Instead of plying the waters off the Atlantic coast seizing enemy ships, American vessels were ordered to take the war overseas to the British Isles. The hope was to implant fear in British citizens that they were not safe from attack, and to force Britain to shift men and ships from America to Europe. This gave Jones the chance to carry out bold raids and engage enemy warships. He took full advantage of the opportunity.

Commander of the *Ranger*

In June 1777 Jones took command of the eighteen-gun ship, *Ranger.* Early the next year he guided her across the Atlantic

One of the Revolution's first naval heroes, John Paul Jones proudly stands aboard a battleship.

idea, quickly agreed to the mission. "When an enemy thinks a design against them is improbable," he later wrote, "they can always be surprised and attacked with advantage."[38]

On April 10, 1778, Jones weighed anchor for England. Fortune smiled upon the American officer, as he quickly captured without a fight the 250-ton ship, *Lord Chatham,* and sank a second schooner. Nearing the British coast, Jones then embarked on a series of hit-and-run raids against British towns and villages.

He was familiar with the target of his initial raid—the town of Whitehaven near his old stomping grounds. Jones assumed that the harbor would likely contain shipping he could attack, and he thought that his knowledge of the region would improve the mission's chances for success.

On April 22 he led two boatloads of men ashore. Ordering one group to burn ships along the shore, Jones took a second unit toward the nearby fort; they scaled the walls by climbing on each other's shoulders, and destroyed the heavy guns. When Jones returned to the harbor, instead of finding ships ablaze, he learned that the other sailors had spent the evening drinking in a pub. An irate Jones started to set fire to a ship as his crew headed back to the boats, but a crowd of

into Quiberon Bay, France, where the ship received the honor of becoming the first American vessel to receive a foreign salute when French warships fired their guns in tribute. Jones then met with the American representative in Paris, the venerable Benjamin Franklin, who proposed that Jones take the *Ranger* into British waters and bring the war directly to English soil. Jones, who intended to push for that townspeople gathered to extinguish the fire. Jones, alone, stood on the pier with his pistol drawn and dared anyone to approach. He had no takers. "After all my people had embarked [in their boats], I stood upon the pier for a considerable time, yet no persons advanced."[39] The image of a solitary Jones holding off a group of hostile civilians while his men rushed to safety enhanced the officer's reputation and solidified the notion that he was one of the Revolution's first heroes.

Jones led his men in a second raid against nearby St. Mary's Isle, where the Lord and Lady Selkirk owned a spacious estate. Instead of allowing his men to destroy the place, Jones demanded the crew act with courtesy and departed after seizing a few valuables. Most of those Jones

later returned to Lady Selkirk. With his own money he retrieved a silver plate collection seized from the estate and sent it back to Lady Selkirk with a letter of apology.

The raids in Britain had little strategic value, for nothing of military importance stood at these targets. Jones knew, as did Franklin, that even a minor attack on a sleepy coastal village produced shock waves that would reverberate throughout the British nation. After the raids Jones said, "What was done is sufficient to show that not all their boasted navy can protect their own coast, and that the scene of distress which they have occasioned in

Jones made many raids on small English ports, such as this one, during April 1778.

America may soon be brought home to their own shores."[40] His ploy worked. Following the raids, numerous towns and villages along Britain's coastline demanded protection from the British government.

A Quick Victory over the British

Jones experienced his first sea battle on April 24, when he engaged the British warship *Drake* in a furious contest off the coast of England. The commander of the *Drake* at first thought the approaching vessel was a friendly ship and dispatched an officer on a rowboat to contact the captain. As soon as the British officer stepped aboard, Jones had him detained below, then turned toward the *Drake*.

While English civilians watched from ashore, Jones and the British captain exchanged cannon shots for a little over an hour. Then, with the *Drake* in ruins and her captain among those killed, the British surrendered. Jones took the ship and her 133 prisoners and made a hasty retreat to France, since he knew that other British warships would be scouring the waters for him.

Jones spent one year in France waiting the arrival of a new ship with which he could again attack the enemy. In that time, he mingled with French society and made numerous acquaintances among famous Americans, including renewing his friendship with Benjamin Franklin. Jones, a strict, demanding officer at sea who expected his officers to dress as immaculately as he, surprised people with his peaceful manner ashore. Future first lady Abigail Adams wrote after meeting Jones, "From the intrepid character he justly supported in the American Navy, I expected to have seen a rough, stout, warlike Roman—instead of that I should sooner think of wrapping him up in cotton wool, and putting him in my pockets, then sending him to contend with cannonballs. He is small of stature, well proportioned, soft in his speech, easy in his address, polite in his manners, vastly civil."[41]

Adams may have been impressed with Jones—he proved to be enormously popular with the ladies of France—but Franklin had a word of advice for his friend. Hearing reports of Jones's sternness at sea, his temper, and his sometimes abrasive personality toward his men, Franklin urged that he soften his manner. "Hereafter, if you should observe an occasion to give your officers and friends a little more praise than is their due, and confess more fault than you can justly be charged with, you will only become the sooner for it, a great captain. Criticizing and censuring almost every one you have to do with, will diminish friends, increase enemies, and thereby hurt your affairs."[42]

As was his custom, Jones failed to heed the advice. Instead, he had more important things to consider, such as heading once more to sea. He had just been given command of another ship, the vessel in which he would gain his greatest fame.

The *Bonhomme Richard*

The forty-gun *Le Duc du Duras* was the largest ship Jones commanded. He renamed the vessel the *Bonhomme Richard* in honor of Benjamin Franklin, who among his many activities had published an eighteenth-century best-seller called *Poor Richard's Almanac*. Jones then set about molding its 380-man crew into a unit. Many were eager to strike at the British, including a seaman named John Kilby, who had been previously captured and mistreated by the British. "Revenge sometimes is quite pleasing to man. We believed Jones would not disappoint us in our great wish and desire."[43]

Jones proved worthy of Kilby's faith. Before departing France, Jones muttered a remark that has been used by American naval officers for the past two hundred years. "I intend to go in harm's way,"[44] he told associates.

On the moonlit night of September 29, 1779, off Flamborough Head on England's east coast, Jones encountered a

A plaque shows the crew of the Bonhomme Richard *with Jones at its crest.*

British convoy heading toward the North Sea. Escorting the ships was the fifty-gun frigate *Serapis.* As the merchant vessels hastened toward shore and safety, the *Serapis* challenged the ship to determine its allegiance. "What ship is that?" the British captain Richard Pearson yelled. Jones replied, "Come a little nearer and I will tell you."[45] With that, Jones ordered the American flag run up the mast.

The *Serapis,* with its larger complement of guns, had the early advantage. Jones hoped to maneuver closer so his guns could be more damaging, but the British cannon kept him at bay by hammering the *Bonhomme Richard*'s masts and hull. Finally, a shift in the wind enabled Jones to inch close enough toward his foe that Jones could order grappling irons tossed over to the British ship. The British cut away many of the irons, but when a huge mast crashed from the *Serapis* into the *Bonhomme Richard,* the vessels were locked together. American sharpshooters killed British sailors stationed in the masts of the *Serapis,* then crossed over from their own masts' tops to those of the enemy and directed fire below.

For over two hours the battle raged in the moonlight. So many cannonballs smashed into the ships that crewmen wondered how long either could remain afloat. Opposing gun crews fired from such close range that sometimes American gun muzzles touched those of the British. Large portions of the hulls and decks were shot away, explosions hurled wooden splinters in all directions, five feet of water splashed below decks on the *Bonhomme Richard,* and fires raged. Some of Jones's guns were so old that they exploded when fired, leaving dead and dying Americans on the deck.

Jones Ups the Ante

Seeing all the bloodshed and damage to his opponent's ship, Captain Pearson shouted out a demand that Jones surrender. The American commander replied with another phrase that has gone down in American naval history: "I have not yet begun to fight!"[46]

As the battle continued, a French ship that had accompanied Jones to British waters and then become separated, now returned to add her cannon to the conflict. Unfortunately, the French captain moved alongside the wrong ship and mistakenly began firing at the *Bonhomme Richard.* Sailors aboard the American vessel shouted in dismay as friendly cannonballs crashed through the hull and mangled seamen while they worked.

Before long, however, an American sailor stationed in the *Serapis*'s mast dropped a grenade below that bounced down a hatchway and ignited clumps of powder that had been scattered about the British guns. The ferocious explosion hurled bodies and limbs all around and killed twenty sailors. Those who survived stood dazed in the smoke and confusion, wearing nothing but the collars of their shirts, since everything else had been blown away.

Now certain that he could resist no longer, Captain Pearson asked for a volunteer to go out on deck to remove the British flag in a gesture of surrender. When no one stepped forward to brave the American fire, Pearson himself performed the task.

Jones's Bonhomme Richard *and the British* Serapis *come head-to-head in one of the most famous naval battles of the American Revolution.*

The End of the Battle

Jones's iron determination to triumph had won the day, but both captains had lost about half of their crews, and both ships were badly damaged. Mangled and burned bodies lay in every corner of both vessels, blood ran everywhere, and cries of the wounded pained the ears of the survivors. One crew member wrote that

so much devastation lay about both decks "to appall the stoutest heart. Upon the whole, I think this battle and every circumstance attending it minutely considered, may be ranked with propriety the most bloody, the hardest fought, and the greatest scene of carnage on both sides, ever fought between two ships of war of any nation under heaven."[47]

In the peculiarities that exist in warfare, the two commanders who had only moments before been engaged in trying to kill one another, now acted with utmost civility. When Captain Pearson offered his sword in surrender, Jones refused and stated that Pearson would be honored by his king for the bravery he exhibited this day. The two leaders then retired to Jones's quarters to drink a few glasses of wine.

The *Bonhomme Richard* had suffered such extensive damage that Jones knew she would sink within the next few days.

Captain Jones stands victoriously aboard the Serapis, *the site of the British surrender.*

Thus he transferred his command to the *Serapis* and arrived in a Dutch port on October 3, having eluded eight British ships sent to capture him. When he arrived in France in February 1780, he received a hero's welcome.

Jones had lost his ship—the gallant *Bonhomme Richard* sank two days after the battle—but he had won a major victory for the American cause. At a time when people in America had grown accustomed to hearing about battlefield losses or lack of supplies, Jones brought them a much-desired triumph that boosted morale. On the basis of this victory, Jones's reputation in history had been secured.

Later Service

Jones returned to the United States in 1781, when a grateful nation gave him command of the country's first seventy-four-gun ship of the line, *America,* then under construction. When the Revolution ended before the ship could be brought into service, Jones returned to France to negotiate payment for ships seized during the war. In recognition for his accomplishments, in 1787 Congress honored Jones with a gold medal.

In 1788, without a war to occupy him, Jones traveled

to Russia, where he accepted a commission as rear admiral from the ruler, Catherine the Great. He performed with distinction against Turkey in the Black Sea, then resigned in 1790 after having a dispute with fellow officers and after being charged in the rape of a woman.

Jones retired to France that same year, where he resided in poor health until his death on July 18, 1792. His body was buried and lay in an unmarked grave until 1905, when it was exhumed and shipped to the United States. In 1906, President Theodore Roosevelt officiated a ceremony at the Naval Academy in Annapolis, Maryland, where the navy interred Jones's body in a tomb in the chapel. On the tomb, an inscription reminds visitors of what Jones, considered the Father of the American Navy, did for his nation—"He gave to our navy its earliest traditions of heroism and victory."[48]

Other posthumous honors came his way. In 1925 he was elected to the Hall of Fame for Great Americans in New York City. Across the Pacific another nation, Japan, hung his picture on the walls of their naval academy along with the images of two other naval heroes—Japanese admiral Heihachiro, victor over the Russians in the Russo-Japanese War—and Lord Horatio Nelson, the esteemed British commander who helped defeat French dictator Napoleon.

Some might wonder why a man who fought two naval battles, only one of them major, deserved such renown. He could hardly control the number of engagements in which he fought, and when the opportunity arose, he made the most of it. Jones provided an answer before he died. "My own opportunities in naval warfare have been but few and feeble. But I do not doubt your ready agreement with me if I say that the hostile ships and commanders that I have thus far enjoyed the opportunity of meeting, did not give anyone much trouble thereafter."[49]

Chapter 6

Benedict Arnold: Betrayer of a Nation

Through the years, the name Benedict Arnold has become synonymous with treachery. Had his attempted betrayal of his fellow American soldiers succeeded, there is no telling what amount of harm it might have done to Washington and the war effort. As is usually the case, a close examination of Arnold shows that he was a more complex man than the popular image suggests. He will, however, justifiably live with a tarnished reputation, for he tried to hand over his nation for money and attention.

A Troubled Youth

Benedict Arnold was born on January 14, 1741, in Norwich, Connecticut, in a family whose ancestors included a four-time governor of Rhode Island. Their distinguished pedigree notwithstanding, however, the family had its share of unhappiness. As a youth, Arnold lost two of his sisters to yellow fever, and his father, also named Benedict, spent much of his time either at work or in one of the local taverns. Thus Arnold relied on his mother, Hannah Waterman King, for direction; he was also very close to his sole remaining sibling, Hanna.

Arnold studied history, Greek, Latin, mathematics, and theology at a private school in Canterbury, Connecticut, for two years but had to return to Norwich at age thirteen when his father's business collapsed. The senior Arnold then began drinking more heavily, forcing his wife to bear the burdens of keeping the family together, in part through the money generated by their farm.

Perhaps because of his erratic home life, the youthful Benedict Arnold frequently landed in trouble. To gain attention from classmates and town friends, he loved pulling pranks, such as jumping completely over moving wagons. He gained the adulation of many teenagers, and the condemnation of numerous adults, by frequently swimming out to a local waterwheel, climbing up on one of the arms, and riding the device while it immersed him in the water.

When the unruly teen challenged the local constable to a fight, Hannah Arnold arranged for her son to be an apprentice in the merchant and drug shop of her two cousins, Daniel and Joshua Lathrop. For eight years Arnold learned how to run a business, spent time at sea on one of the Lathrop ships, and, above all, gained an

Benedict Arnold is best known for his betrayal of America.

appreciation for fine living. The Lathrops, one of Norwich's wealthiest families, lived in a stately mansion maintained by slaves. Arnold enjoyed the elevated lifestyle and planned to match it when he was older.

First, military duty beckoned. In 1757, the sixteen-year-old Arnold joined the Norwich militia during the French and Indian War, when the French advanced toward Massachusetts. He packed his few belongings, said goodbye to his mother and friends, and marched out to do battle; but before he arrived at the scene of the fighting, the French had retreated from the region. He would have to wait to prove his mettle in battle.

When his mother died three years later, Arnold experienced harsher times. His father's drinking worsened, and the teenage Arnold frequently had to search Norwich's taverns to bring his father home. In 1761 Arnold's father died a broken man, leaving the family farm to his son, Benedict.

A Successful Merchant

Arnold completed his apprenticeship (training) under the Lathrops in 1762. With some money given him by relatives, Arnold opened a store in New Haven, Connecticut, where he planned to cater to the growing population of students at Yale University. Rarely worried about the state of his finances, Arnold sailed to London, where he used credit to buy the best items he could find to stock the store. He sent to New Haven a stream of jewelry, stationery, pictures, maps, Bibles, surgical instruments, drugs, and books, confident that the ever-present body of students would provide a steady market for his materials.

For a time the profits bankrolled a high standard of living, allowing Arnold to reside in a mansion, ride through New Haven's streets in an elegant carriage, and earn the admiration of many citizens. But when he could not make payments on an overextended line of credit, he landed in debtors' prison for six weeks. On this occasion, and indeed throughout his life, Arnold created problems for himself by spending more than he made.

Arnold corrected his money woes by selling the family farm, purchasing three ships, and bringing his sister, Hanna, to New Haven to run the store while he headed to sea. Arnold's ships brought numerous items into the colonies, and even quietly slipped into open harbors with smuggled goods to evade the king's duty collectors and avoid paying what most colonists considered excessive taxes.

A depiction of the 1770 Boston Massacre in which British soldiers killed a group of American colonists.

Once again Arnold, now esteemed and called Captain by his peers, enjoyed a luxurious standard.

His life appeared to be settling into a happy course in 1767 when he married Margaret Mansfield, the daughter of the local sheriff. The couple eventually had three sons, whom Arnold largely neglected. In 1775 Margaret died and Hanna, the boys' aunt, took over the parental duties.

As revolutionary activity increased in the New England colonies, Arnold became an enthusiastic partisan. He wrote newspaper articles condemning the king's taxes on imported goods and joined the rebel organization Sons of Liberty. Following the Boston Massacre, when British soldiers shot and killed a group of colonists, Arnold wrote to a friend, "Good God, are the Americans all asleep & tamely giving up their glorious liberties, or, are they all turned Philosophers that they don't take immediate vengeance on such miscreants?"[50]

Militia Command Granted, Then Removed

In December 1774 New Haven formed its own militia. It was customary to ask one of the town's most prominent citizens to command the unit, and the people turned to Arnold. He relished preparing his men for battle, and after news of the war's opening battles at Lexington and Concord in April 1775, he advocated a quick strike against the British. Opposed by many of his New Haven peers, who voted to keep the town neutral, Arnold led his militia toward the ammunition shed and forced officials to open it to him. He then took his men toward Cambridge, outside Boston, where Arnold hoped to meet with other American forces for an attack against the British.

At Cambridge, Arnold immediately proposed a daring assault against Fort Ticonderoga, a key location in New York, since in British hands it both protected Canada from an American advance and offered an invasion route into the colonies. Arnold argued that the British defenders had grown so lax in their vigilance that he could readily seize it, and its much-needed cannon and other supplies, from the small garrison. The Massachusetts Committee of Public Safety—with prominent individuals such as Sam Adams and Joseph Warren—agreed, appointing Arnold a colonel and ordering him to lead four hundred men toward the fort.

Arnold had no sooner commenced his march when he learned that Vermont had sent Ethan Allen and a group of militia on a similar expedition. Arnold and Allen met at a Vermont tavern to discuss the operation, and though the two were cool toward each other and each wanted to retain overall command, they agreed to compromise and work together.

On the night of May 9–10, Arnold and Allen led their men in a surprise assault against Ticonderoga. Caught unawares—the British commander still had not donned his pants—the British handed over the fort without a fight. When the British officer handed over his sword to Allen, Arnold felt slighted.

Arnold gained more distinction with two subsequent actions in New York. On May 12 he helped seize the British fort at Crown Point, and five days later, using ships that eventually evolved into the first elements of the United States Navy, he surprised the garrison at St. John. Though he later had to abandon the fort when British reinforcements approached, Arnold returned to Massachusetts with three victories in hand.

But instead of a rousing welcome, Arnold faced criticism and scorn. In the official report of the campaign, Ethan Allen failed to hand any credit to Arnold, even though the Connecticut man had served with distinction as a co-commander. Bitter over that omission, Arnold then successfully battled charges by the Massachusetts state legislature that he had grossly exceeded the limits of the approved finances and diverted funds for his own purposes as well. When his superiors named another man to assume command of Arnold's militia, Arnold angrily disbanded the group and resigned. The incident was only the first in a line of events that embittered Arnold and nudged him toward drastic action.

Colonels Benedict Arnold (center) and Ethan Allen take Fort Ticonderoga in May 1775.

Hero in Canada

Within a few months, Arnold was once again eager to command troops. He gained his opportunity with the 1775 invasion of Canada, where he led troops under the supervision of Major General Philip Schuyler. The plan called for two thrusts into Canada, one heading north up Lake Champlain while a second, under Arnold, wound through the forests of Maine toward Quebec.

Arnold and 1,000 men, including 250 sharpshooters with the words "Liberty or death" stitched on their caps or the fronts of their shirts, boarded ships in September. Once landed in Maine, the force faced three hundred miles of harsh terrain, including winding valleys, raging streams, and dense forests. Rain and sleet so slowed the men that they soon began running out of food. The weakened men resorted to eating candles, dogs, and shoe leather. By November 2, two hundred men had perished. One man wrote that the survivors, who still faced miles of marching, "were so weak that they could hardly stand on their legs. I passed by many sitting wholly drowned in sorrow. Such pity-asking countenances [faces] I never before beheld. My heart was ready to burst."[51]

After coming across a French settlement and food, Arnold's replenished men waited for the second force to arrive near Quebec. Now led by General Richard Montgomery, who had taken over because Schuyler fell ill, the two units joined on December 2. Arnold made a fa-vorable impression on Montgomery, who wrote Schuyler that "I find Colonel Arnold's corps an exceeding fine one, inured to fatigue. There is a style among them much superior to what I have used to see in this campaign."[52]

Montgomery and Arnold marched on Quebec, where they sent in a message to the British commander, General Sir Guy Carleton, demanding his surrender. Carleton quickly tossed the note into a fire and counted on Canada's frigid winter and his town's sturdy defenses to stop the Americans.

In a blinding snowstorm on New Year's Eve, Montgomery and Arnold led their men in a coordinated charge against Quebec. Hard fighting engaged opposing soldiers in many of the town's homes, but the Americans yielded ground when their two leaders fell, Montgomery fatally and Arnold with a wound to his leg. The invaders retreated after losing more than four hundred men as prisoners.

Arnold, now in overall command, continued the siege of Quebec until June. Then, threatened by the arrival of British reinforcements, he ordered a retreat to Massachusetts. Along the way, he managed to obtain numerous commodities for his personal use, actions that raised eyebrows in many circles. Some suspected bribery; others claimed that Arnold forced local businessmen to sell to him at exorbitant low prices. The nineteen-year-old Aaron Burr, later a vice president of the United States, respected Arnold's courage in battle but condemned the man for his lack of morals. "He is utterly unprincipled and has no love of country or self-respect to guide him," he wrote a friend. "He is not to be trusted anywhere but under the eye of a superior."[53]

Despite the loss at Quebec and the suspicions of unethical financial activities, Arnold had enough friends in the Continental Congress to gain a promotion to brigadier general. He now stood ready to meet another challenge in battle—this time on the water against the British.

Glory in New York

In the fall of 1776, General Horatio Gates ordered Arnold to construct a fleet of small boats to use on Lake Champlain against a reported English fleet. Arnold cleverly placed his ships between the mainland and Valcour Island, in a narrow channel that he knew would permit only a portion of the larger British fleet to enter. When the two units opened fire on each other on October 11, 1776, Arnold had the advantage of numbers, but the superior training of the British navy carried the day. By nightfall the British, having heavily damaged Arnold's fleet, retired with the intent to finish the task on the next day.

They had not counted on the skill of their adversary. Arnold banned speaking and ordered his ships to extinguish their lights. Then, hidden by darkness and

Prior to Arnold's attack in January 1776, British ships wait patiently near Quebec during the Seven Years' War.

heavy fog, with Arnold in the lead vessel, the battered ships sailed quietly past the British. The next morning the British chased after Arnold and sank some of his ships, but the American had managed to extricate the bulk of his men. He had lost the battle at Valcour Island, but in sinking some of the British ships, he forced the enemy to retreat to Canada and delayed the invasion of New York until the next spring. By then, the Americans were better prepared to meet the threat.

Arnold expected to receive another promotion, but instead, in February 1777, Congress advanced five other officers above him. Insulted, Arnold demanded an investigation and threatened to resign, but George Washington talked him out of it and promised to write letters to officials in Arnold's behalf.

A brave exhibition against the British at Danbury, Connecticut, where Arnold had his horse shot out from beneath him, led the Continental Congress to finally promote Arnold to major general. Arnold could not completely rejoice in the occasion, however, since Congress also refused to reimburse him for the expenses he had claimed. Unable to document these expenses, he had argued that Congress should accept his word as an officer. The legislature declined to do this, and Arnold again believed he had been slighted. He grew more bitter toward his fellow officers and complained that he was not receiving the honors and esteem to which he was entitled.

The Battle of Saratoga

Arnold's next piece of glory occurred in the battle considered to be the turning point of the Revolution—Saratoga. In the September 19 fighting around Freeman's Farm, the first of two clashes that comprised Saratoga, Arnold orchestrated a stout defense in which he skillfully massed sharpshooters at one end of the battle line and Continental soldiers in the middle. When British general John Burgoyne's forces advanced, Arnold seemed to be everywhere, encouraging his men and shouting commands. Three different times Arnold came close to repelling the British, but he lacked sufficient troops to complete the task. Repeated requests to his superior, General Horatio Gates, went unheeded. Arnold later contended that if Gates had sent him the needed troops, the colonists could have won the battle.

That night the two sides dug in and waited for a more opportune moment to attack. In the interval, Arnold and Gates argued so heatedly over the lack of reinforcements that Gates confined Arnold to his tent and ordered him out of the coming second engagement, which unfolded on October 7. Listening to the sounds of battle, Arnold fretted about missing the action that swirled about Bemis Heights. Finally, unable or unwilling to remain at his tent, Arnold disobeyed orders, leapt onto his horse, shouted "Victory or death!"[54] and rode toward the fighting.

His disregard for Gates's command proved beneficial to the Americans, as

Arnold rallied the weary Americans to take two main British positions. At one point in the fighting, he rode directly across a field, in plain view of the British, to join with a group of soldiers and lead them against two cabins defended by the enemy. Largely due to Arnold, who fell to a leg wound, the Americans defeated Burgoyne and caused the surrender of one of the largest groups of British soldiers in the war.

Like most of his previous actions, what could have been a moment of triumph instead turned to bitterness when Burgoyne handed his sword of surrender to Gates, who happened to be the senior American commander. Arnold sulked about what he

"Do Your Duty!"

As Benedict Arnold rallied the Americans at Bemis Heights, he spotted an equally brave British officer encouraging his men from his horse. Arnold quickly realized the value this officer, General Simon Fraser, had to his men, so he ordered his sharpshooters to focus their efforts on Fraser.

As Robert Leckie relates in his book, *George Washington's War,* Arnold told another officer, "That man on the gray horse is a host in himself, and must be disposed of!" Arnold then turned to one of the best sharpshooters, Tim Murphy, and added, "That gallant officer is General Fraser. I admire him, but it is necessary that he should die—do your duty!" Murphy's first two shots nicked Fraser's horse, but the British general refused to take shelter from the inevitable third shot. This time, Murphy struck Fraser in the chest and knocked him out of the battle. The British officer died later that night.

considered another slight and told friends he wished the bullet that had struck his leg had instead smacked into his heart.

More Problems

Arnold's death wish may have intensified as he recuperated from his wound. First of all, General Gates failed to mention his younger colleague's name in his official report of the fighting at Saratoga. Then, opponents pressed serious charges, including accusations that he had permitted his men to illegally loot Montreal. At the trial held in Philadelphia, Arnold brashly challenged each officer on the court-martial board to a duel, but Gates stepped in before harm could be done and ordered the court disbanded for lack of evidence against the defendant.

Washington, who had always stood in Arnold's corner, offered the injured leader the post of military governor of Philadelphia. On June 19, 1778, he took command, then immediately implemented several controversial steps that caused concern in many of the city's inhabitants. Arnold, using his position of power, purchased hard-to-find goods at a low price, then resold them at an enormous profit. While citizens chafed under wartime conditions, Arnold rode in a beautiful carriage and lived in an elegant mansion.

Once again Arnold faced a list of charges, this time from the state of Pennsylvania. Adding insult to injury, Pennsylvania sent copies of the charges to newspapers and to the other state gov-

Arnold (center) is wounded in the leg during the Battle of Saratoga.

ernments. Arnold was so incensed at this action that he resigned from his post in February 1779 and demanded a trial. "For heaven's sake," he pled, "let me be immediately tried and, if found guilty, executed. I want no favor. I only want justice."[55] He was cleared of all charges except misusing wagons for personal gain, but as punishment he received a written reprimand from Washington.

Soured by the repeated accusations and by being frequently passed over when praise was apportioned for military actions, Arnold wondered if his services might be better appreciated by the British. When in April 1779 he married Margaret "Peggy" Shippen, the daughter of a judge who remained loyal to the king, Arnold had more reason to move to the other side, for his bride equally loved fine living and hated the Revolution.

"Treason of the Blackest Dye"

The British encouraged American officers to switch allegiance by offering large sums of money. Knowing this, Arnold contacted a friend of his wife's, Major John Andre, who was serving as an aide to British general Henry Clinton. Informed by Andre of the offer, Sir Henry Clinton told his subordinate to proceed cautiously in case the move was a trick.

Andre asked Arnold for proof that he could be of value to the British. On May 21, 1779, the American sent information about the troops' movements, then asked for money to cover the losses he expected to incur by changing sides. The British, still dubious, next requested that Arnold divulge details of the strategic position at West Point, a fort on the Hudson River that guarded the approach to New York City. Arnold agreed, and soon had persuaded Washington to appoint him commander of the important fort.

"I have accepted the command at West Point as a post in which I can render the most essential services, and which will be in my disposal," Arnold wrote Andre on July 12, 1780. "The mass of people are heartily tired of the war and wish to be on their former footing."[56] He then purposely weakened the fort's defenses by spreading out his soldiers instead of massing them at important locations and by sending men out to chop wood instead of strengthening the fort.

Finally, on September 21, 1780, Arnold and Andre met clandestinely near West Point to arrange the final details. Unable to return to the ship that had brought him to the rendezvous, Andre tried to make his way over land back to British lines. Three American soldiers stopped him, performed a search, and discovered a document hidden in one sock.

The soldiers turned over Andre and the note outlining the defenses at West Point, to an officer, who promptly notified Washington. Unaware of Arnold's involvement, the officer also sent word to West Point's soon-to-be-former commander of the seizure. The American, realizing he would be implicated, fled to the British only moments before Washington arrived to arrest him.

Andre was tried and found guilty of spying, an offense punishable by hanging. Washington offered to exchange the British major for Arnold, but Clinton declined the offer because he wanted to encourage more Americans to defect. On October 2, 1780, Major Andre was hanged.

"Treason of the blackest dye was yesterday discovered," American general Nathanael Greene stated on September 26. "General Arnold, who commanded at West Point, lost to every sentiment of honor, of public and private obligation, was about to deliver up that important fort into the hands of the enemy. Such an event must have given the American cause a deadly wound if not a fatal stab. Happily the scheme was timely discovered to prevent the final misfortune."[57]

Arnold faced scorn from both the English as well as the Americans he betrayed. Clinton, never trusting a man who could so readily switch sides, was further angered with the execution of his aide. He never permitted Arnold to command in any important campaign. Arnold led minor raids into Virginia and Connecticut, but his military career would go no further.

Arnold became the object of scorn and hatred. Americans hanged him in effigy, and Philadelphia citizens placed a dummy representing Arnold in a wagon,

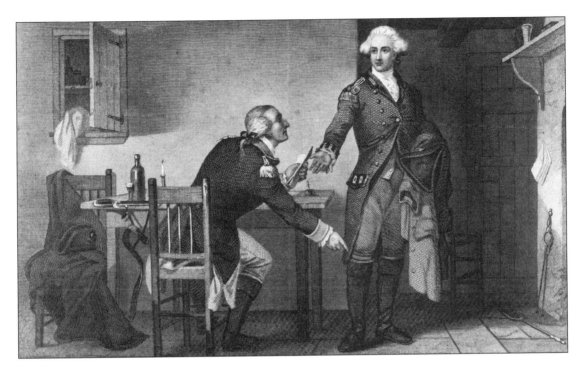

Benedict Arnold and John Andre secretly meet on September 21, 1780. Andre was later hanged and Arnold disgraced as an American traitor.

placed an image of the devil next to him, and paraded it through the city streets. When one American officer was captured and brought to him, Arnold asked him what Americans would do if he were caught. "If my countrymen should catch you, I believe they would first cut off that lame leg which was wounded in the cause of freedom and virtue, and bury it with the honors of war; and afterwards hang the remainder of your body in gibbets, high."[58]

Return to England

Arnold found little happiness after the Revolution. With the British defeat at Yorktown, he and Peggy sailed for England in hopes of living in peace, but the British treated them with a cool reserve.

Hated in America, Arnold now felt distant from former friends in England, who preferred to avoid a man known for betraying his country.

The couple eventually moved to St. John, Canada, and then to the West Indies, where Arnold attempted to rebuild his merchant business. When that failed, they once more returned to England. Deep in debt and shaken with almost constant coughing and asthma, Arnold died in London on June 14, 1801, two years before his wife passed away.

Chapter 7

The Able and Arrogant Cornwallis

Possibly the most talented general to serve the British during the American Revolution was Charles Cornwallis. He commanded with competence and flair, and almost succeeded in trapping Washington's army before the Battle of Trenton. In the end, however, his name has become associated with surrender and loss.

A Pleasant Beginning

Cornwallis was born on December 31, 1738, in Suffolk, England, to illustrious parents. His father, Charles, bore the titles of the fifth Baron of Eye and the first Earl and Viscount Brome, while his mother, Elizabeth, was the daughter of one of England's most prominent political leaders, Lord Townshend, and the niece of Robert Walpole, a great prime minister. In 1661 Cornwallis's grandfather, Frederick, had been honored for faithful service by King Charles II, and one of his uncles rose to the powerful post of Archbishop of Canterbury.

Like many other children born to luxury, Cornwallis attended the nation's elite schools. At Eton, an exclusive preparatory school, he learned to be tough and flexible. In those days upperclassmen habitually roughed up underclassmen like Cornwallis, but the young man readily adapted to what was almost a lawless atmosphere. Following his time at Eton, Cornwallis entered the famed Cambridge University.

In 1756, at the age of seventeen, Cornwallis entered the military with the First Regiment of Foot, an infantry unit. Showing the seriousness with which he conducted himself throughout life, Cornwallis then traveled to Turin, Italy, to be schooled at a renowned military academy. Many of his contemporary officers who enjoyed important connections, as did Cornwallis, did little to further their military knowledge, but Cornwallis wanted to absorb as much as possible before being entrusted with men's lives in combat.

While at Turin, Cornwallis received orders to join his unit for duty in the Seven Years' War. In 1758 he served as the aide-de-camp (assistant) to the Marquis of Granby, one of England's foremost military officers, where he gained valuable knowledge in the art of command. By 1761 Cornwallis had shown such talent in leadership and boldness in action, particularly at the 1759 Battle of Minden, that he had been promoted to lieutenant colonel.

To North America

With his father's death in 1762, Cornwallis returned to England to assume the duties as the next earl. He finalized his father's estate, then took his hereditary seat in the House of Lords. Cornwallis had not been involved in politics as student or soldier, but with events in North America heating up, he now took an active interest.

On most issues he sided with the colonists, who he believed had been overly taxed. In 1765 he voted to repeal the Stamp Act, which placed heavy duties on various everyday items, and the next year voted against the Declaratory Act, which stated the king of England was supreme in all political matters governing the colonies. Despite voting against the king, Cornwallis remained a royal favorite,

British general Charles Cornwallis studied at this military academy in Turin, Italy.

probably because of his illustrious family. In 1765, for instance, King George II named Cornwallis his aide-de-camp, and the following year Cornwallis rose to the rank of colonel in the Thirty-third Regiment of Foot.

As shown by his willingness to learn the military trade at Turin and his opposition to the king, Cornwallis exhibited a refreshing independence of thought and action. He showed this again in 1768, when he married Jemima Jones, the daughter of a military officer with no influential connections. He loved her, and that was all that mattered to Cornwallis. The couple lived in Brome Hall in Suffolk at the family estate, where they eventually became the parents of one son and one daughter.

In December 1775 Cornwallis, now a lieutenant general, was ordered to sail for America. After a difficult Atlantic Ocean crossing that lasted five months, Cornwallis served as deputy for Major General Henry Clinton during a failed June 1776 attempt to capture Charleston, South Carolina. After this inept performance by British troops, Cornwallis sailed north to join the main effort in New York.

Service in New York and New Jersey

Cornwallis commanded the reserve force in New York, a relatively minor post. He used it to his advantage, however, by ably supporting General Clinton's advance at the August 22, 1776, Battle of Long Island, where Cornwallis repeatedly led his troops forward against heavy fire. These and other actions in which Cornwallis participated helped shove Washington out of New York toward New Jersey and Pennsylvania.

After this engagement, Cornwallis experienced anguish and elation in trying to corner the Continental army led by George Washington. He rode almost fifty miles nonstop to take command of British forces in New Jersey after the Americans' stunning victory at Trenton, then stumbled in his initial encounter with Washington. On January 2, Cornwallis detached one brigade of soldiers as a rear guard in nearby Princeton, then led the remaining troops south toward Trenton. Cornwallis had an opportunity to order an immediate attack on the weary Americans, camped just across a small creek, but he decided to give his own exhausted men time to regroup.

This handed Washington a chance to outmaneuver his opponent. When Cornwallis heard the usual camp noises and spotted fires in the American position, he assumed Washington's men had settled in for the night and decided against sending out nighttime patrols. One officer advised that Cornwallis take immediate action against Washington rather than wait until the next day, but Cornwallis replied, "Nonsense, my dear fellow. We've got the old fox safe now. We'll go over and bag him in the morning. The damned rebels are cornered at last!"[59]

Far from being cornered, however, Washington, under cover of darkness,

Cornwallis's troops mount a disastrous offensive at the Battle of Long Island.

slipped around Cornwallis's side to strike at Cornwallis's rear guard in Princeton. Muffling the sounds of movement by covering the wagon wheels with rags, Washington quietly headed north to Princeton and another bold victory. The blow succeeded in knocking the British off balance so much that Cornwallis had to fall back to New Brunswick, even farther north.

Cornwallis redeemed his honor the following September when he commanded troops at the victory against Washington along Brandywine Creek. General Sir William Howe ordered Cornwallis to take two-thirds of the British soldiers, march seventeen miles around Washington's right flank, and launch an attack on the American rear. While he did this, another group of British infantry held American forces along the Brandywine with continuous shelling.

Cornwallis made a striking figure. One man later wrote that the British officer "was on horseback, appeared tall and sat very erect. His rich scarlet clothing loaded with gold lace, epaulets, etc., occasioned him to make a brilliant and martial appearance."[60]

Washington countered by fortifying a position around the Birmingham Meeting House directly in Cornwallis's path. Hours of battle, which included repeated bayonet charges and hand-to-hand combat, finally forced the Americans out of their positions.

Cornwallis was known for his authoritative demeanor and elegant dress.

Hopes for Higher Command

Cornwallis's first eighteen months in America had proven valuable to him and to his country. He earned high marks for his battlefield conduct and familiarized himself with the British high command. On December 16, 1777, Cornwallis returned to England, a man with an apparently bright future.

In England, he cared for his wife, who was ill, and appeared in Parliament, but after a few months Cornwallis sailed back to America. Before long, he was once again facing the formidable George Washington. As the British army headed toward New York City from Philadelphia, Washington unleashed an attack at Monmouth, New Jersey. In command of the rear guard, Cornwallis successfully counterattacked and repelled Washington's attempt. This battle so weakened the American forces in the northern colonies that, for the rest of the war, most of the fighting occurred in the South.

News from home called Cornwallis back to England. His beloved wife had taken a turn for the worse, and in November 1778 Cornwallis hastened to be at her side. Jemima died in February, however, and a crushed Cornwallis journeyed once more to America, hoping to immerse his sorrow in a flurry of military activity. As he explained in a letter to his brother, William, "I am now returning to America, not with view of conquest & ambition, nothing brilliant can be expected in that quarter; but I find this country [England] quite unsupportable to me. I must shift the scene. I have many friends in the American Army [the British in America]. I love that Army, & flatter myself that I am not quite indifferent to them."[61]

Cornwallis was especially upbeat about returning to the scene of his prior military successes because the current commander in chief, General Henry Clinton, had been threatening to resign his position unless he received more support from England. Such a move would open the path for someone else to take over, not inconceivably Cornwallis himself.

Indeed, in 1780, during operations in South Carolina, Clinton discussed many of his strategic plans with Cornwallis in case the latter were to succeed him as commander in chief. This preparation for a change in command that might not happen, however, was to have a negative effect on Cornwallis, for he started to act as if the promotion were assured.

Yet his chances appeared even better when he and Clinton, after a harsh three-month siege, took Charleston in May 1780. Along with the city, they captured the largest stock of ammunition, supplies, and horses of the entire war. Then, perhaps assuming that the need for more support from England had passed, the king declined to accept Clinton's offer to resign.

Upon learning this, a demoralized Cornwallis turned on his commander, even angrily blaming him for his not receiving a promotion. Cornwallis wrote an associate that since Clinton had "now come to a resolution to remain in the country, my services here must necessarily be of less consequence."[62]

Conflict in the South

Cornwallis changed his opinion when Clinton, ready to depart for New York, appointed him to lead the British forces in the South. Eager to attain more glory, Cornwallis attempted to create a group of soldiers and subordinate officers who were devoted to him. He gathered a circle of promising junior officers, including the feared cavalry leader, Lieutenant Colonel Banastre Tarleton, and favored them with choice assignments. Cornwallis allowed the soldiers to plunder American homes and businesses in South Carolina, which may have been

Under General Gates (center), American fighters proudly defend the Carolinas from Cornwallis.

welcome by the regular British soldier but was angrily denounced not only by rebel sympathizers, but also by those who had been wavering.

One colonist wrote of Cornwallis's march that "like a desolating meteor he has passed, carrying destruction and distress to individuals—his army walked through the country, daily adding to the number of its enemies, and leaving their few friends exposed to every punishment for ill-timed and ill-placed confidence."[63]

On August 16, 1780, Cornwallis again met the Americans at Camden, this time led by General Horatio Gates. In under one hour Cornwallis had routed Gates so thoroughly that the defeated commander fled from the field of battle.

This easy win caused Cornwallis to assume he had events under control in the South. He viewed the hit-and-run tactics used by American guerrilla leaders, especially Francis Marion, Thomas Sumter, and Daniel Morgan, as ineffective and not requiring his full attention, a misjudgment that would later have drastic effects.

When Morgan inflicted a stinging loss on Tarleton at the Cowpens, near the North Carolina border, on January 17, 1781, an angry Cornwallis leaned on his sword so hard that he snapped the blade. Hoping to forestall criticism of his command by London officials, Cornwallis headed out in pursuit of Morgan. Joined by the able general, Nathanael Greene, Morgan and the Americans eluded every

trap Cornwallis tried to set and fled across the Dan River. Again, Cornwallis's troops plundered and burned homes and buildings along the route. The tactic might have been sound militarily, since it denied the supply source to the Americans, but it solidified anti-British sentiment among the people who saw their belongings destroyed.

Cornwallis pressed on, intending to force Greene and Morgan to fight. Unaccountably, he believed that the British, outnumbered almost four to one, could handily defeat a force whose training he still scorned. If he could wrest a victory from Greene and Morgan, Cornwallis felt confident his reputation would be secure, despite the setbacks at the Cowpens and in the futile pursuit to the Dan.

He found what he looked for on March 15, when he encountered Greene's forces aligned in three formations at Guilford Court House, North Carolina. Cornwallis sent his fifteen hundred men in a bayonet charge against the forty-four hundred Americans. The British advanced against no opposition until they closed within forty yards of the Americans when, according to a British officer present, "both parties surveyed each other for the moment with the most anxious suspense." After the brief pause, the British moved forward to the urgings of their officers, "Come on, my brave fusiliers!"[64]

The king's troops charged directly into such a withering American fire that the attack faltered in the heavily forested

Cornwallis's zealous pursuit of victory over the American troops often led him to risk his life and to cause many British casualties.

area. So determined to attain victory was Cornwallis that he endangered his own life to lead the men. Twice, horses were shot out from underneath him, and Cornwallis received a slight wound. Opposing soldiers closed in on each other to grapple among the bushes and trees in fighting that some compared to the worst the French and Indian War had ever offered.

In a desperate move to prevent the onrushing Americans from overwhelming his retreating British, Cornwallis ordered a volley fired directly into the mass of soldiers. The move stopped the American offensive, although it also killed many

British soldiers. The British held the field at the Guilford Court House, but they lost so many men that Cornwallis's superiors were hard put to call it a victory.

Pursuit of Lafayette

Still hoping to gain a decisive triumph in the South, Cornwallis shifted the scene of operations to the Chesapeake region of Virginia. Most of May 1781 consisted of

Cornwallis again in pursuit of his foe, now under the leadership of the French officer, the Marquis de Lafayette. The two armies came close to engaging, but Lafayette, knowing himself to be the weaker, always eluded the British, thus avoiding certain defeat. However, he had to at least put on a display of military force, as much to maintain loyalty among the civilians as to perplex Cornwallis. As Lafayette wrote Washington on May 24, "Were I to fight a battle, I should be cut to pieces, the militia dispersed, and the arms lost. Were I to decline fighting, the country would think itself given up. I am therefore determined to skirmish, but not to engage too far, and particularly to take care against their immense and excellent body of horse, whom the militia fear as they would so many wild beasts."[65] At first confident of capturing Lafayette, Cornwallis became more doubtful as the slippery French commander avoided trap after trap.

When the commander of the British navy in America mentioned he required a stronghold along the Atlantic coast into which he could safely winter his fleet, Cornwallis suggested a town along the Chesapeake Bay, Yorktown, as the base from which the army could conduct protective operations once the fleet sailed into the bay.

Cornwallis began fortifying Yorktown in August 1781. His superiors wanted the defenses at Yorktown speedily constructed, since rumors had come in that the French navy, now allied with the Americans, would soon appear in force. But Cornwallis failed to convey a sense of urgency to his men, and the fort's defenses rose only slowly. When at the end of August a French ship was spotted, Cornwallis ordered an immediate increase in activity, but it was too late.

On September 2 the French started landing troops across the peninsula from Yorktown. When Washington converged on the area from the north, Cornwallis ordered all his men to fall back to the fort rather than keep some in outlying strongholds. This allowed Washington to move closer to the town and concentrate his artillery on the congested collection of British troops.

The Americans now orchestrated one of the most intense bombardments of the war. In one twenty-four-hour span, the Americans fired more than thirty-six hundred cannonballs against Yorktown, which rattled as if struck by an earthquake. Soldiers fled their tents in panic, British ships blazed from direct hits, and the town's inhabitants rushed to the waterfront to evade a fiery death. On October 11, Cornwallis wrote Clinton that the bombardment, which had not stopped for two days, would soon reduce him to impotence unless help arrived from New York.

By October 15, Washington had so tightened the lines about Yorktown that Cornwallis feared little could save him. Now living in an underground bunker, he rushed a dispatch to superiors stating that

General Washington (center, right) surveys the American-French stronghold at Yorktown before the Patriots' crushing defeat of the British.

it might not be worth the risk to send a relief force into the area.

Surrender at Yorktown

Cornwallis attempted one final move to save his men. During the night of October 15, he collected as many small craft as could be found in hopes of removing his soldiers by sea, but a ferocious storm shattered any chances of success.

Two days later, after an inspection of the front lines, Cornwallis sent a messenger to Washington asking for a cease-fire. A solitary British drummer dressed in red climbed to one of the highest points of Cornwallis's line and beat the sound indicating the commander wished to talk. With a bombardment in progress, the Americans could not hear the drummer, but they understood the message being conveyed.

On October 19, six thousand British soldiers, some with tears running down their cheeks, marched out of Yorktown while a military band appropriately played the tune "The World Turned Upside Down." Cornwallis was not present to lead his men out of the fort—lamely avoiding the public humiliation of surrender, he pled illness as an excuse to be absent. The Americans confined British soldiers to Virginia and Maryland prison

General Cornwallis (left) surrenders to General Washington (right) at Yorktown, thereby ending the American Revolution.

camps, while Cornwallis and his staff were first feasted by Washington's officers, then permitted to return to New York on the promise of not fighting again.

British leaders in England reacted to the news with disbelief. The prime minister, Lord North, paced back and forth in his residence shouting, "Oh God! Oh God! It is over! It is all over!"[66]

Cornwallis and Clinton engaged in a heated debate over who should bear the blame for Yorktown, the last major battle of the war. He continued to defend himself when he sailed back to England in

January 1782, where he found considerable support among political allies.

After the Revolution

Cornwallis received important posts following the American Revolution. In 1785 he was assigned as an envoy to the court of Frederick the Great of Prussia (now a part of Germany). Appointed governor general of India in 1786 and promoted to the rank of field marshal, Cornwallis sailed to the subcontinent, determined to bring order to a land rent with strife and intent on establishing British rule. He worked tirelessly to reorganize the Indian infrastructure, introducing a system of taxation that reduced the opportunities for corruption and dividing India into twenty-three administrative districts.

Cornwallis also had to once again employ his military talents to put down a rebellion fomented by an Indian aristocrat, Sultan Tippoo Sahib. Leading a combined British-Indian army, Cornwallis defeated the sultan in 1792 to end the strife. The next year, weary of his labors, Cornwallis headed for England.

When fighting erupted in Ireland in 1798, the British government dispatched Cornwallis to put down that rebellion as well. As Lord Lieutenant of Ireland, Cornwallis crushed the rebellion orchestrated by Wolfe Tone.

In 1802, having represented his country in peace negotiations with the French dictator Napoleon, Cornwallis, now in his mid-sixties and in frail health, returned to his country estate to live out the remainder of his years. When unrest again plagued India, the British government coaxed the reluctant Cornwallis out of retirement in 1805, but within a few months of arriving in India, Cornwallis died on October 5 from a fever. Out of a mark of respect for what the British officer did for the country, Cornwallis's grave overlooking the Ganges River is today maintained by the Indian government.

☆ Chronology of Events ☆

1722

February 2: John Burgoyne is born in England.

1727

July 26: Horatio Gates is born in England.

1729

August 10: William Howe is born in England.

1732

February 22: George Washington is born in Virginia.

1738

December 31: Charles Cornwallis is born in England.

1741

January 14: Benedict Arnold is born in Connecticut.

1747

July 6: John Paul (Jones) is born in Scotland.

1754

July 3–4: George Washington fights the battle at Fort Necessity.

1758

William Howe inherits a seat in Parliament when his brother dies.

1759

September 18: William Howe serves with distinction in the Battle of Quebec.

1775

February: William Howe takes command of the British army in America; John Burgoyne arrives in America.

May 9–10: Benedict Arnold helps seize Fort Ticonderoga.

May 12: Benedict Arnold takes Crown Point.

May 17: Benedict Arnold takes St. John.

June 17: The British capture Bunker Hill.

July 3: George Washington arrives in Boston to take command of the Continental army.

December 31: Benedict Arnold fails to take Quebec.

1776

March 17: George Washington forces William Howe to pull out of Boston.

August: The Battle of Long Island is fought.

September 16: The Battle of Harlem Heights is fought.

October 11: Benedict Arnold escapes from the British at the Battle of Valcour Island.

December 7: John Paul Jones is commissioned a lieutenant in the Continental navy.

December 26: Washington surprises the Hessians at Trenton.

1777

January 3: George Washington defeats Howe at Princeton.

July 6: Fort Ticonderoga is taken by the British.

April 22: John Paul Jones leads a raid against Whitehaven.

April 24: John Paul Jones, in the *Ranger,* captures the British ship *Drake.*

September 11: The Battle of Brandywine is fought.

September 19: The Battle of Freeman's Farm, part of the monumental clash at Saratoga, is fought.

October 4: The Battle of Germantown is fought; the Battle of Bemis Heights, part of the monumental clash at Saratoga, is fought.

October 17: John Burgoyne surrenders at Saratoga.

Winter 1777–1778: Washington and the Continental army endure a bitter winter at Valley Forge.

1778

June 28: The Battle of Monmouth Court House is fought.

1779

May 21: Benedict Arnold begins sending secret information on American moves to the British.

September 29: John Paul Jones commands the *Bonhomme Richard* in a classic sea duel against the British ship *Serapis.*

1780

August 16: Horatio Gates is soundly defeated at the Battle of Camden.

1781

March 15: Charles Cornwallis wins a costly victory at Guilford Court House.

October 19: Charles Cornwallis surrenders at Yorktown.

1786

Charles Cornwallis is appointed governor general of India.

1788

John Paul Jones starts a two-year term as a rear admiral in the Russian navy.

1789

April 30: George Washington takes the oath of office to become the first president of the United States.

1792

July 18: John Paul Jones dies in Paris.

August 3: John Burgoyne dies in London.

1793

March 4: George Washington is sworn in for a second term as president.

1798

Charles Cornwallis suppresses a rebellion led by Wolfe Tone in Ireland.

1799

December 14: George Washington dies.

1801

June 14: Benedict Arnold dies in London.

1805

October 5: Charles Cornwallis dies in India.

1806

April 10: Horatio Gates dies in New York City.

1814

July 12: William Howe dies in Plymouth, England.

1906

The U.S. Navy inters the body of John Paul Jones in a tomb in the Annapolis chapel.

☆ Notes ☆

Chapter 1: George Washington: Man for All the People

1. Quoted in A.J. Langguth, *Patriots.* New York: Simon and Schuster, 1988, p. 295.
2. Quoted in George Athan Bilias, ed., *George Washington's Generals.* New York: William Morrow, 1964, p. 10.
3. Quoted in Langguth, *Patriots,* p. 382.
4. Quoted in Henry Steele Commager and Richard B. Morris, eds., *The Spirit of 'Seventy-six.* Indianapolis: Bobbs-Merrill, 1958, p. xvi.
5. Quoted in Langguth, *Patriots,* pp. 413–14.
6. Quoted in Marcus Cunliffe, *George Washington and the Making of a Nation.* New York: American Heritage, 1966, p. 76.
7. Quoted in Cunliffe, *George Washington and the Making of a Nation,* pp. 109–10.
8. Quoted in Cunliffe, *George Washington and the Making of a Nation,* p. 123.
9. Quoted in James Thomas Flexner, *Washington: The Indispensable Man.* Boston: Little, Brown, 1974, p. 318.

Chapter 2: William Howe: Hesitant Leader

10. Quoted in Robert Leckie, *George Washington's War.* New York: Harper-Perennial, 1992, p. 147.
11. Quoted in Page Smith, *A New Age Now Begins.* New York: McGraw-Hill, 1976, p. 503.
12. Quoted in Smith, *A New Age Now Begins,* p. 531.
13. Quoted in George Athan Bilias, ed., *George Washington's Opponents.* New York: William Morrow, 1969, p. 47.
14. Quoted in Benson Bobrick, *Angel in the Whirlwind.* New York: Simon and Schuster, 1997, p. 165.
15. Quoted in Bobrick, *Angel in the Whirlwind,* p. 166.
16. Quoted in Bilias, *George Washington's Opponents,* p. 65.
17. Quoted in Lt. Col. Joseph B. Mitchell, *Discipline and Bayonets.* New York: G.P. Putnam's Sons, 1967, p. 74.
18. Quoted in Bobrick, *Angel in the Whirlwind,* p. 311.
19. Quoted in Bilias, *George Washington's Opponents,* p. 40.

Chapter 3: Horatio Gates: Hero or Villain?

20. Quoted in Bilias, *George Washington's Generals,* p. 82.
21. Quoted in Bilias, *George Washington's Generals,* p. 84.

22. Quoted in Christopher Ward, *The War of the Revolution*. New York: Macmillan, 1952, p. 384.

23. Quoted in Leckie, *George Washington's War*, p. 399.

24. Quoted in Leckie, *George Washington's War*, p. 407.

25. Quoted in Bilias, *George Washington's Generals*, p. 95.

26. Quoted in Bilias, *George Washington's Generals*, p. 97.

27. Quoted in Leckie, *George Washington's War*, p. 530.

28. Quoted in Commager and Morris, *The Spirit of 'Seventy-six*, p. 1,135.

Chapter 4: John Burgoyne: The Dashing General

29. Quoted in W.J. Wood, *Battles of the Revolutionary War, 1775–1781*. Chapel Hill, NC: Da Capo Press, 1995, p. 133.

30. Quoted in Bilias, *George Washington's Opponents*, p. 153.

31. Quoted in Mitchell, *Discipline and Bayonets*, p. 45.

32. Quoted in Mitchell, *Discipline and Bayonets*, p. 46.

33. Quoted in Leckie, *George Washington's War*, p. 399.

34. Quoted in Wood, *Battles of the Revolutionary War, 1775–1781*, pp. 163–64.

35. Quoted in Leckie, *George Washington's War*, p. 416.

Chapter 5: John Paul Jones: Hero of the Seas

36. Quoted in Samuel Eliot Morison, *John Paul Jones*. Boston: Little, Brown, 1959, p. 15.

37. Quoted in Morison, *John Paul Jones*, p. 19.

38. Quoted in Stephen Howarth, *To Shining Sea*. New York: Random House, 1991, p. 36.

39. Quoted in Smith, *A New Age Now Begins*, p. 1,270.

40. Quoted in Jack Sweetman, ed., *Great American Naval Battles*. Annapolis, MD: Naval Institute Press, 1998, p. 34.

41. Quoted in Bobrick, *Angel in the Whirlwind*, p. 387.

42. Quoted in Howarth, *To Shining Sea*, p. 35.

43. Quoted in Nathan Miller, *The U.S. Navy*. New York: American Heritage, 1977, p. 27.

44. Quoted in Howarth, *To Shining Sea*, p. 39.

45. Quoted in Smith, *A New Age Now Begins*, p. 1,276.

46. Quoted in Howarth, *To Shining Sea*, p. 39.

47. Quoted in Bobrick, *Angel in the Whirlwind*, p. 390.

48. Quoted in Sweetman, *Great American Naval Battles*, p. 45.

49. Quoted in Howarth, *To Shining Sea*, pp. 41–42.

Chapter 6: Benedict Arnold: Betrayer of a Nation

50. Quoted in Bobrick, *Angel in the Whirlwind*, p. 135.

51. Quoted in Bobrick, *Angel in the Whirlwind*, p. 171.

52. Quoted in Wood, *Battles of the Revolutionary War, 1775–1781*, p. 47.

53. Quoted in Bobrick, *Angel in the Whirl-wind*, p. 405.
54. Quoted in Leckie, *George Washington's War*, p. 412.
55. Quoted in Willard Sterne Randall, *Benedict Arnold: Patriot and Traitor*. New York: William Morrow, 1990, p. 452.
56. Quoted in Commager and Morris, The *Spirit of 'Seventy-six*, p. 748.
57. Quoted in Commager and Morris, *The Spirit of 'Seventy-six*, p. 755.
58. Quoted in Bobrick, *Angel in the Whirl-wind*, p. 422.

Chapter 7: The Able and Arrogant Cornwallis

59. Quoted in Langguth, *Patriots*, p. 426.
60. Quoted in Leckie, *George Washington's War*, p. 352.
61. Quoted in Bilias, *George Washington's Opponents*, p. 201.
62. Quoted in Bilias, *George Washington's Opponents*, p. 203.
63. Quoted in Bilias, *George Washington's Opponents*, p. 223.
64. Quoted in Bobrick, *Angel in the Whirl-wind*, p. 431.
65. Quoted in Bobrick, *Angel in the Whirl-wind*, p. 442.
66. Quoted in Bobrick, *Angel in the Whirl-wind*, p. 466.

⭐ For Further Reading ⭐

Richard Goldstein, *Mine Eyes Have Seen.* New York: Simon and Schuster, 1997. Goldstein collects first-person accounts of major historical events in United States history. Ten of those included pertain to the American Revolution.

Joy Hakim, *From Colonies to Country.* New York: Oxford University Press, 1993. Hakim's book contains numerous portraits of important Revolutionary War events and leaders. This is a fine place to start researching the conflict.

Phillip Hoose, *We Were There, Too! Young People in U.S. History.* New York: Farrar Straus Giroux, 2001. Hoose has written one of the most fascinating history books available. The volume contains stories by and about young people who were involved in different events in United States history, including a chapter covering the American Revolution.

Bonnie Lukes, *The American Revolution.* San Diego: Lucent Books, 1996. Lukes's book presents a superb survey of the American Revolution for junior high school students. Outstanding text is complemented with helpful illustrations.

Norma Jean Lutz, *Benedict Arnold: Traitor to the Cause.* Philadelphia: Chelsea House, 2000. Lutz has written a lively account for upper elementary students of the Revolutionary War's greatest villain. The book contains numerous illustrations to assist the reader.

———, *John Paul Jones: Father of the U.S. Navy.* Philadelphia: Chelsea House, 2000. Like her companion volumes on Benedict Arnold and George Washington, this biography of Jones presents a brief overview of the naval officer's career.

———, *George Washington: First U.S. President.* Philadelphia: Chelsea House, 2000. Lutz has written a decent account of our first president that should appeal to upper elementary students.

Linda R. Monk, *Ordinary Americans: U.S. History Through the Eyes of Everyday People.* New York: Close Up, 1994. This excellent collection of first-person accounts contains a superb chapter dealing with the Revolution. Both junior high school and high school students will enjoy this volume.

Brendan Morrissey, *Boston 1775.* Oxford: Osprey, 1993. Morrissey's book includes many colorful illustrations of British and American uniforms and weapons used during the Revolutionary War. The text is written for the high school level, but the illustrations and accompanying maps are helpful to anyone.

Wendie C. Old, *George Washington*. Springfield, NJ: Enslow, 1997. Elementary students will find this account helpful. Old attempts to portray all the important events of Washington's life.

★ Works Consulted ★

George Athan Bilias, ed., *George Washington's Generals*. New York: William Morrow, 1964. Bilias assembles an excellent collection of biographical essays on Washington's leading commanders. The chapter on Gates is especially valuable.

———, *George Washington's Opponents*. New York: William Morrow, 1969. The companion piece to his earlier work, Bilias again delivers a superb collection of biographical chapters detailing the contributions of British commanders.

Benson Bobrick, *Angel in the Whirlwind*. New York: Simon and Schuster, 1997. A very readable account of the fighting of the American Revolution. The book contains decent portraits of the main commanders, plus descriptions of the battles.

Henry Steele Commager and Richard B. Morris, eds., *The Spirit of 'Seventy-six*. Indianapolis: Bobbs-Merrill, 1958. Two esteemed historians combine forces to give a unique examination of the Revolution, consisting entirely of the personal accounts of men and women who lived during the Revolution. They include accounts written by the well-known leaders, such as Washington, as well as letters penned by the ordinary soldier or merchant.

Marcus Cunliffe, *George Washington and the Making of a Nation*. New York: American Heritage, 1966. This book has been a solid source on Washington for four decades. Numerous paintings and maps supplement this easy-reading volume.

James Thomas Flexner, *Washington: The Indispensable Man*. Boston: Little, Brown, 1974. Flexner has written one of the best one-volume biographies of Washington. He blends powerful descriptions with organized writing to bring Washington to life.

Stephen Howarth, *To Shining Sea*. New York: Random House, 1991. British naval historian Howarth surveys the history of the United States Navy in this very readable volume. His comments on John Paul Jones are valuable and insightful, and his descriptions of battle at sea are helpful for understanding Jones's contributions.

A.J. Langguth, *Patriots*. New York: Simon and Schuster, 1988. The author has cleverly told the story of the American Revolution through the lives of the chief American military contributors.

He thus includes much material on Washington, Arnold, and Gates.

Robert Leckie, *George Washington's War.* New York: HarperPerennial, 1992. Military historian Leckie tells the story of the American Revolution largely through the eyes of George Washington. The technique works well, and Leckie is potent in his battlefield descriptions.

Nathan Miller, *The U.S. Navy.* New York: American Heritage, 1977. Numerous paintings, maps, and photographs supplement a fine text in this general overview of American naval history. John Paul Jones's contributions receive ample recognition.

Lt. Col. Joseph B. Mitchell, *Discipline and Bayonets.* New York: G.P. Putnam's Sons, 1967. West Point graduate and historian Mitchell presents biographical portraits of ten top revolutionary commanders, including Washington, Burgoyne, and Cornwallis. The easy-reading chapters are filled with helpful information.

Samuel Eliot Morison, *John Paul Jones.* Boston: Little, Brown, 1959. Morison, one of the most revered naval historians of the last century, has given us the definitive biography of Jones. His meticulous research and outstanding writing style guarantee that this biography will be the standard for years to come.

Willard Sterne Randall, *Benedict Arnold: Patriot and Traitor.* New York: William Morrow, 1990. This biography is one of the most valuable accounts available of a controversial subject. The author attempts to present the evidence on Arnold, then allows readers to form their own conclusions why Arnold betrayed his country.

Page Smith, *A New Age Now Begins.* New York: McGraw-Hill, 1976. This two-volume work forms an important part of Smith's monumental multivolume history of the United States. He includes numerous quotes from participants to liven the narrative.

Jack Sweetman, ed., *Great American Naval Battles.* Annapolis, MD: Naval Institute Press, 1998. Editor Sweetman presents nineteen famous American battles at sea, each written by a distinguished historian. Two chapters that helped for this book are those covering Valcour Island and Flamborough Head.

Christopher Ward, *The War of the Revolution.* New York: Macmillan, 1952. Ward's work is justly considered by historians to be a classic of writing. This indispensable source provides a powerful examination of all aspects of the Revolution.

W. J. Wood, *Battles of the Revolutionary War, 1775–1781.* Chapel Hill, NC: Da Capo Press, 1995. The author presents ten crucial battles of the Revolution, including chapters on Bunker Hill, Trenton, and Saratoga. The book offers a superb place to learn the basic information about these conflicts.

☆ Index ☆

★ Picture Credits ★

⭐ About the Author ⭐

John F. Wukovits is a junior high school teacher and writer from Trenton, Michigan, who specializes in history and biography. Besides biographies of Anne Frank, Jim Carrey, Stephen King, and Martin Luther King Jr. for Lucent, he has written biographies of the World War II commander Admiral Clifton Sprague, Barry Sanders, Tim Allen, Jack Nicklaus, Vince Lombardi, and Wyatt Earp. A graduate of the University of Notre Dame, Wukovits is the father of three daughters—Amy, Julie, and Karen.